King David put his pen to parchment sending a morally and politically corrupt America a clear warning: "If the foundations be destroyed what can the righteous do?"

Vicki Shearin, in her latest book, *Sodom or Salem?*, has taken a moral and spiritual snapshot of America and what we must do as righteous people to reclaim and rebuild our moral and spiritual foundation. *Wake up America!*

- **John Hagee**, Senior Pastor of Cornerstone Church, San Antonio, TX. *New York Times* bestselling author of *Four Blood Moons* and *Jerusalem Countdown,* founder and national chairman of Christians United for Israel

Sodom or Salem? – A choice that Americans will make at the polling place, and that will depend on Christians deciding to no longer be the "silent" majority.

> **- Mac Hammond**, Senior Pastor of Living Word Christian Center, Brooklyn Park, MN and host of the *Winner's Way* broadcast and author of several internationally distributed books.

My dear friend Vicki writes with such rhythm and grace. Her attention to details that are real and will affect our lives as well as our nation are plainly laid out, creating a must-read to remain watchful and prayerful in this season of change.

> **-Lynne Hammond**, Bible teacher, publisher of a newsletter called *Prayer Notes*, author of numerous books, and national prayer director for Daughters for Zion.

Sodom or Salem? America, It's Your Choice is a wake up call to our nation at a critical moment. As you read how Vicki was stirred out of complacency to take a close look at the deceptive ways of thinking currently being accepted as truth, you too will be moved to action. This book is definitely written "for such a time as this." It is time for people who love America to rise to pray, to be informed, to speak out, and to extend love, compassion, hope and healing for broken people in our nation and in the world. Vicki Shearin offers a clear voice from the truth of God's unchanging word to give us direction and light in the midst of darkness.

I enjoyed reading Vicki Shearin's new book, *Sodom or Salem?* Vicki has her hand on the pulse of modern society and God's word. In this work, she shares challenging words for challenging times. What I especially appreciate about this book is its candid, realistic assessment of the days in which we live, but even more than that, its clear call to godly, biblical, and loving action. Believers must fulfill their function as salt, as light, and as Christ's ambassadors. *Sodom or Salem? America its Your Choice* challenges us to be all that God has called us to be as agents of hope and redemption in this world.

Sodom or Salem? America, it's Your Choice is a powerful and very timely publication. Never before in history has the Church so needed to wake up and speak out. This book offers believers an invigorating challenge, and Vicki Shearin does so with a message that grips the heart. It is time to take heed and change the direction in which our country is headed. Will it be *Sodom or*

Salem? Thank you, Vicki, for hearing God's voice and relaying this pertinent message.

> **- Janet Boynes**, inspirational speaker, and author of *Called Out, A Former Lesbian's Discovery of Freedom* and *Arise*.

AMERICA, IT'S YOUR CHOICE

VICKI SHEARIN

I dedicate this book to my beloved friend,
Cynthia Watson,
whose prayers and encouragement I have
always been able to count on.

Acknowledgments

There are so many people to thank for helping me get this book written and published, but I especially want to acknowledge three groups of people: First, my husband, David, and daughter, Ashley, who have been a constant source of love, support, and inspiration; secondly, my friends and mentors in ministry who have "been there" for me and my family – Pastors Ken and Lynette Hagin, Pastors Phil and Barbara Privette, and everyone who blessed me with their endorsement of the book, especially my dear friends Mark and Trina Hankins, who, for years, have believed in me, invited me to speak at their conferences, and encouraged me to write; thirdly, our Word of Life Christian Center and David Shearin Ministries staff and volunteers who helped with this project by editing, researching, fact-checking, cover design and advising, namely, Ty Ward, Keyanna Stewart, Lisa Cash-Hanson, Shelli Hadley, Samantha Jones, Ashley Shearin and Destinee Thames. I also want to thank the leadership of Ladies LIFE*styles* and everyone in my wonderful church family who have supported me with their prayers! I could not have done it without you. I appreciate you all and love you very much!

Contents

Chapter 1
My Wake-Up Call

Exhausted, I dropped my head on my pillow and curled up under the covers for a much-needed good night's rest. It was just after eleven p.m. on a Thursday in the spring of 2004. As I was drifting off to sleep, I was suddenly awakened by a voice asking, "Sodom or Salem?" My eyes popped open to a dark room. I sat up in bed, a bit stunned. My husband David wasn't home from the office yet, and being a school night, our thirteen-year-old daughter Ashley was upstairs in her bedroom sleeping. The voice I heard was loud enough to arouse me from slumber!

My husband David and I met in 1979 in Tulsa, Oklahoma while attending Rhema Bible Training College (RBTC) - jokingly known as "Rhema *Bridal* Training College." Three months after our wedding in 1982, we moved to Las Vegas to pioneer a church. I'm from a small town in Iowa and David is from a small town in North Carolina. (I fell in love with his southern accent and his southern gentleman's manners!) This pair of small-town newlyweds embarked on two life-altering journeys: marriage and ministry... in Las Vegas, no less.

In spite of the unique challenges of pastoring a church in what is infamously known as "Sin City," we love what we do! Our work is our passion and the rewards are outstanding: unbelievers find faith in God, the broken-hearted are healed, drug addicts are delivered, marriages are restored, and tragedies are turned into triumphs - all because of God's amazing grace! Still, needless to say, we've had to make a few adjustments along the way.

For example, we've learned that it's important to take a day off once a week to spend some relaxing time together. I know that isn't a novel idea - it's actually one of the Ten Commandments! But we had to learn its value and necessity the hard way, so we've chosen Friday as our "day off." In order to make that happen, we often work long hours during the week, and sometimes David works late into the evening on Thursdays. This particular Thursday, in the spring of 2004, he worked extra late, so I went to bed before he got home.

Sodom or Salem?

I sat alone in bed, pondering what I'd heard. I realized that although it seemed audible, what I actually heard was the voice of God speaking to my spirit. I also realized that the question *"Sodom or Salem?"* was not posed exclusively to me - it was as if I heard God demanding a choice from America.

I had just finished teaching a series of messages in the church on "Homosexuality from a Biblical Perspective." I concluded the series with the story of Sodom and Gomorrah. I honestly did not want to teach on the subject anymore, but after I "finished," the Holy Spirit continued to draw me back to the story in the Book of Genesis.

I knew Sodom was one of the cities God destroyed. And Salem? Hmm, that's a city too, right? I wondered: is there a verse or a passage in the Bible that includes both of these words,

I mean both of these cities? I reached over to turn on the lamp by my bedside, but my Bible was not on my nightstand where I sometimes leave it. Still groggy, I didn't feel like getting up out of bed, so I opened my nightstand drawer, found a piece of paper, and wrote down: *Sodom or Salem?* As I turned the light out, I muttered a promise to God: "I will look into this tomorrow." Very soon I was back to sleep.

TGIF! And what a beautiful Friday it was! We Las Vegans enjoy sunshine approximately 350 days out of the year, but in the spring temperatures are in the mid-70s, and this morning was perfect for jogging with my Labrador. About two blocks into my exercise route, I began inquiring of the Lord as to what He meant by waking me up with *Sodom or Salem?* "What does this mean?" I asked, not really expecting an answer at the moment. But it came immediately: *"It's the title of a book.....that you're going to write."*

This time it was just the still, small voice I was accustomed to hearing on occasion, but I believe I was more stunned to hear this than I was to hear *Sodom or Salem?* the night before! It would be years before I would even tell David that I was supposed to write this book. I have known that God called me to write since I was a teenager, but I had not yet written a book (only gospel tracts and one "mini-book"), and I felt so unqualified to tackle a subject like this!

When I finally made it to my study that day to commence my research, I opened my Bible to the Book of Beginnings, Genesis chapter 18 where the story of Sodom and Gomorrah begins. Or does it? In chapter 18, God reveals to Abraham that He will destroy the city of Sodom, and Abraham stands before the Lord to intercede. Not finding Salem in that chapter or the next, I checked my concordance, which directed me back four chapters and approximately 17 years before the infamous destruction of Sodom and Gomorrah by fire and brimstone. Sure enough, there it was: Genesis 14:17-23 speaks of the king of Sodom and the king of Salem.

The Holy Spirit spoke to me again: "I want you to study the characters in the story, beginning with the king." When I shared my experience with David and Ashley later that evening, Ashley said, "I didn't even know there was a king of Sodom." Honestly, I hadn't thought much about it either. The characters that typically come to mind are Abraham, Lot, the Angels, and, of course, "remember Lot's wife!"

I was about to discover, and never forget, that there was indeed a king of Sodom - Bera was his name. The time was approximately 3200 BC - the Bronze Age. As civilizations began to evolve, kings reigned over city-states. And King Bera's role in the story of Sodom and Gomorrah was quite significant.

In Genesis chapter 13, when Abraham (then called Abram) and his nephew, Lot, outgrew their property (their flocks and herds were so abundant that their herdsman were quarrelling with each other), Abraham told his nephew to separate from him and generously offered him first choice of the expansive land before them. "If you take the left," Abram said, "I will go to the right; or, if you go to the right, I will go to the left."

Lot chose for himself all the plain of Jordan, which included these cities: Sodom, Gomorrah, Admah, Zeboiim, and Zoar. The Bible says Lot chose to journey in this direction because of the prosperity it seemed to promise. The land in this valley was *"well watered everywhere [before the Lord destroyed Sodom and Gomorrah] like the garden of the Lord." (v. 10)*

Note to self: all that glitters isn't gold! *"But the men of Sodom were exceedingly wicked and sinful against the Lord." (Genesis 13:13)* Lot *"pitched his tent toward Sodom" (v. 12)*, and eventually he was living there.

After Lot moved down into Sodom, a war broke out – the first recorded war in Scripture. The sub-heading for Genesis chapter 14 in my Bible reads:

"The Battle of Four Kings Against Five"

King Chedorlaomer of Elam (Elam is modern day Iran) and his allied forces attacked the king of Sodom and the cities of the plain. The king of Sodom and the king of Gomorrah found themselves fleeing from their enemies, who prevailed in capturing the people of Sodom and plundering all the goods. While fleeing, both King Bera of Sodom and King Birsha of Gomorrah fell into slime pits.

Upon hearing that Lot had been taken captive, Abraham promptly armed his 318 servants (the original "Israeli Defense Force") and set off to rescue his nephew. He accomplished his mission and more - he overtook King Chedorlaomer, recovering all the people and all the goods of Sodom. Next is the Bible's first mention of tithing and the passage where I found both words (both cities): Sodom and Salem:

> And the king of Sodom went out to meet him (Abraham) at the Valley of Shaveh (that is, the

King's Valley), after his return from the defeat of Chedorlaomer and the kings who were with him. Then Melchizedek king of Salem brought out bread and wine; he was the priest of God Most High. And he blessed him and said: "Blessed be Abram of God Most High, Possessor of heaven and earth; And blessed be God Most High, Who has delivered your enemies into your hand." And he gave him a tithe of all. Now the king of Sodom said to Abram, "Give me the persons, and take the goods for yourself." But Abram said to the king of Sodom, "I have raised my hand to the LORD, God Most High, the Possessor of heaven and earth, that I will take nothing, from a thread to a sandal strap, and that I will not take anything that is yours, lest you should say, 'I have made Abram rich' — except only what the young men have eaten, and the portion of the men who went with me: Aner, Eshcol, and Mamre; let them take their portion."(Genesis 14:17-24)

A Divine Intervention

Thanks to Abraham and his special forces (318 of his own servants and three Amorite neighbors), the people of Sodom who narrowly escaped death were also spared the bondage of servitude, and King Bera himself was rescued from a slime pit. Immediately following this "special operation," King Bera and the people of Sodom witnessed Melchizedek, king of Salem, show up on the scene and declare to Abraham that it was God Most High who delivered his enemies into his hand.

Next, they had the rare opportunity to witness Abraham, the father of Judeo-Christian faith, present to Melchizedek a tenth of the spoil, demonstrating to King Bera and to all the observing people of Sodom, that God, "Possessor of Heaven and Earth," was the source of his victory and provision.

Salem is the earliest name for Jerusalem, the city of God,[1] which is mentioned over 800 times in the Bible! Melchizedek, king of Salem, is arguably the most outstanding type of Christ in the Old Testament. Of all the amazing types and shadows of Christ throughout every book in the Bible, none typify Christ as profoundly as Melchizedek. Some commentators even suggest he was not a type, but Christ Himself.

The Book of Hebrews tells us to *"consider how great this man was."* Melchizedek's name means *"King of Righteousness."* He was the King of Salem (Jerusalem) - the King of Peace. He was *"without father, without mother, without geology, having neither beginning of days nor end of life, but made like the Son of God."*[2] He brought forth bread and wine, a foreshadowing of Communion, which symbolizes the elements of the New Covenant (Christ's broken body and shed blood for the remission of our sins). The Bible declares seven times that Jesus was made *"a Priest forever after the order of Melchizedek."*[3]

What was King Bera's response to this astonishing divine intervention? One might expect him to fall down before Abraham in humble gratitude. Perhaps he would inquire of Abraham: "What do you know that I don't know?" or exclaim, "Take me to your leader!" Since Abraham paid tithes to Melchizedek, who pronounced a blessing on Abraham, we might expect King Bera to "consider how great this man was!" Instead, King Bera presumptuously and arrogantly tried to cut a deal with Abraham: *"Give me the persons, and take the goods for yourself,"* he bargained. *(Genesis 14:21)*

Abraham could have scoffed at King Bera's offer and claimed all of the spoil - he was clearly the undisputed victor of the battle. He could have even declared himself king by conquest! He certainly assumed rightful ownership when he paid his tithes and let his men eat of the spoil. But Abraham responded to the king of Sodom: *"I have raised my hand to the LORD, God Most High, the Possessor of heaven and earth, that I will take nothing, from a thread to a sandal strap, and that I will not take anything that is yours, lest you should say, 'I have made Abram rich.'" (Genesis 14:22-23)*

Abraham gave all the plunder back to him! In essence he was saying, "Go ahead and take it. I have paid my tithes. I will be fine. God is my source! No one's going to say the government of Sodom made me rich!"

Not surprisingly, God made Abraham very rich!

Who, Me?!

Now here comes the revelation that up-ended my theology and my life's priorities. As I was meditating on this passage where I found both of the words, Sodom and Salem, suddenly the metaphor became painfully clear to me. It was as if the Holy Spirit pointed to me and said, "YOU are the King of Sodom!"

He explained: "You may identify with Abraham if you

want to, and you should, because he is the character of choice in the story. (He was the intercessor on the mountain, far away from the destruction.) But you don't have a choice as to whether or not you will identify with the king of Sodom because America is not a monarchy."

Suddenly it hit me, as they say, like a ton of bricks. I reasoned: King Bera was the ruling force in Sodom, but the government of the United States is a democracy or a republic. I pulled out my Webster's Dictionary and looked up "democracy" and "republic." Democracy is defined as "government in which the people hold the ruling power." A republic is "a state or nation in which the supreme power rests in all the citizens entitled to vote, and is exercised by representatives elected."[4]

The Allegory

I was stunned by this analogy even though it was so simple. Our Founding Fathers established a representative form of government - a government "of the people, by the people, and for the people." Metaphorically, "We the people" are the king!

After the attack on his city, his encounter with Abraham, and his revelation of Christ (Melchizedek), the king of Sodom had a critical choice to make. Would he humble himself and repent for the wickedness in Sodom? Would he change the way he governed his city? Would he enact laws to change the behavior of Sodom's citizens? King Bera had the opportunity, the privilege, and the power to make a difference, but there is no record of him doing any such thing!

The citizens of the United States of America are in the

same position today that King Bera found himself in over 5,000 years ago. Unprecedented prosperity has been ours. We have experienced the goodness of God like no other nation in the world. We have survived numerous wars; in recent years, we have been attacked on our own soil. We have had an encounter with Abraham and Christ – we have been blessed with a tremendous Judeo-Christian heritage. Our nation is now at a crossroads and we are responsible for its future.

Will we choose Sodom or Salem?

Christ
Covenant
Commandment
Creation
Conscience

Chapter 2
Degrees of Light

The question is: How do we avoid Sodom and choose Salem? Believe me, I have sought the Lord earnestly concerning this!

The Hebrew word translated Sodom means "burnt," as in volcanic or bituminous. The meaning of the verb is "to scorch." In contrast, the Hebrew word translated Salem means "peaceful."[1] It carries essentially the same meaning as these Hebrew words: shalem - wholeness, shalam - safety, and shalom - peace. The choice between Sodom and Salem shouldn't be too difficult!

Sodom represents judgment. In the back of my Thompson Chain Study Bible, under Archaeological Supplement, I found this astounding commentary by Dr. George Adam Smith on the ruins of Sodom and Gomorrah:

> Here was laid the scene of the most terrible judgment on human sin. The glare of Sodom and Gomorrah is flung down the whole length of Scriptural history. It is the popular and standard judgment of sin. The story is told in Genesis; it is applied in Deuteronomy, by Amos, by Isaiah, by Jeremiah, by Ezekiel, and Zephaniah, and in Lamentations. Our Lord employs it more than

once as a figure of the judgment He threatens
upon cities where the word is preached in vain,
and we feel the flame scorch our own cheeks
(Matt. 10:15; 11:24; Luke 10:12; 17:29). Paul,
Peter, Jude make mention of it. In Revelation the
city of sin is spiritually called Sodom. Though
the glare of this catastrophe burns still, the ruins
it left have disappeared.[2]

Throughout the Bible, and especially in the passages
about Sodom and Gomorrah, the consistent message regarding
judgment is this: ***Judgment comes when light (truth) is reject-
ed, when warnings go unheeded, and when there is a refusal
to repent.***

The most familiar, most quoted, and most memorized
verse in the Bible is John 3:16:

For God so loved the world that He gave His
only begotten Son, that whoever believes in Him
should not perish but have everlasting life.

Consider what Jesus said in the three verses immediately
following this beloved verse:

For God did not send His Son into the world to
condemn the world, but that the world through
Him might be saved. He who believes in Him
is not condemned; but he who does not believe

is condemned already, because he has not believed in the name of the only begotten Son of
God. And this is the condemnation, that the Light
has come into the world, and men loved darkness
rather than light, because their deeds were evil.
(John 3:16-19)

Verse 19 in the Amplified Bible reads:

The [basis of the] judgment (indictment, the test
by which men are judged, the ground for the sen-
tence) lies in this: the Light has come into the
world, and people have loved the darkness rather than and more than the Light, for their works
(deeds) were evil.

The Light of Conscience

*"This is the message which we have heard from Him and
declare to you, that God is light and in Him is no darkness at
all." (1 John 1:5)*

Everyone has been granted some degree of light (truth/
revelation). The first degree of light that everyone has been
granted is "the light of conscience." The Gospel of John 1:9
says that God gives light to every person coming into this world.
This is the "light of conscience" we are all born with. Although
in our flesh we inherited our sinfulness from Adam, we are born
into this world with spirits that are alive unto God. Babies are

born innocently and instinctively knowing God. This is why Jesus insisted we must become as little children to enter the Kingdom of God.[3]

Once we reach "the age of accountability" and knowingly sin against God (which everyone does), we become spiritually separated from Him;[4] hence, Jesus said we must be "born again."[5] Nevertheless, we are created in God's image and that initial light we are born with leaves an indelible impression upon our souls causing us to instinctively know right from wrong. This is "the light of conscience" that every human being has been granted.

The Light of Creation

Secondly, God has wonderfully granted all of us the "light of creation." Romans 1:20 in the New Living Translation, says,

> For ever since the world was created, people
> have seen the earth and sky. Through everything
> God made, they can clearly see his invisible
> qualities—his eternal power and divine nature.
> So they have no excuse for not knowing God.

God's creation is a revelation and a declaration of His existence and His glory. Consider Psalm 19:1-4, in the New Living Translation:

> The heavens proclaim the glory of God.

The skies display his craftsmanship.
Day after day they continue to speak;
night after night they make him known.
They speak without a sound or word;
their voice is never heard.
Yet their message has gone throughout the earth,
and their words to all the world.

Growing up in Iowa, I enjoyed the splendor of all four seasons: in the Spring, dogwoods budding and daffodils blooming; in the fall, rolling hills blanketed with rich red, orange, and yellow foliage; in the winter, over the river and through the woods to grandmother's house we'd go, braving the icy roads in my dad's never-without Ford truck, seldom ever having to "dream of" a brilliant white Christmas! And in the summer, our family vacationed on Lake Ada in the north woods of Minnesota. There is nothing like waking up to the call of a loon on a glassy lake, bathed in morning sun and surrounded by majestic pines, or sitting on the dock at midnight literally star-struck by the night sky. When we pause to listen, God's creation will speak profoundly to us about Him.

The people of Sodom were all born with the "light of conscience" and they had all been granted the "light of creation." In addition, they knew about the Great Flood. The Sodomites were descendants of Ham, one of Noah's three sons, and some of them were likely born before Noah died or at least before Ham died. The Bible says Noah lived 350 years after the flood and was "a preacher of righteousness."[6] Although they had no written commandments, they had probably been taught about the commandments God gave Noah and the covenant God made with him and his sons after they came out of the Ark.[7] Like you and I observe today, they couldn't miss the sign of the covenant - the beautiful rainbow - appearing in the sky after a thunderstorm. Their wicked behavior was indicative of their rejection of light.

On the other hand, The Book of Job is considered one of the oldest writings of the Bible, perhaps of equal date with The Book of Genesis. It is a poetic masterpiece, extravagantly praised for its literary qualities. More importantly, it is an inspired story of a man of great antiquity named Job, who suffered many personal tragedies and physical afflictions. His "friends" lectured him judgmentally about how he must have sinned and his wife told him to curse God and die. Albeit, Job patiently endured his pain and maintained his integrity and his worship of God (even though God seemed distant, unconcerned, and even to blame for his suffering). Like the Sodomites, Job had no written oracles, but he responded appropriately to the light he had been granted, and acknowledged God the best he knew how.

The climax of the Narrative, which Alfred, Lord Tennyson called the greatest poem of ancient and modern times, is when *"God answered Job out of the whirlwind."*[8] The Creator spoke to Job through His creation. He spoke of His glorious attributes, His unsearchable wisdom, His irresistible power, His impeccable justice, and His incontestable sovereignty. Job's confusion and despair were turned into a more veracious praise of God, as well as compassionate prayers for his friends. God, in turn, restored Job with twice as much wealth and blessing than he had before his afflictions.

The Light of Commandment

God's original Covenant (Agreement) with Adam and Eve included one condition - one "thou shalt not" commandment:

> And the LORD God commanded the man, saying, "Of every tree of the garden you may freely eat; but of the tree of the knowledge of good and evil you shall not eat, for in the day that you eat of it you shall surely die." (Genesis 2:16-17)

When Adam and Eve disobeyed God's commandment, they broke the agreement God made with them. God clearly warned them that the consequence (the judgment or penalty) for their disobedience would be death. Death is not cessation of being; death is separation. Their disobedience immediately resulted in a spiritual separation from God. Physical death was also a result, but didn't occur until hundreds of years later.

The Book of Proverbs warns us twice: *There is a way, which seemeth right unto a man, but the end thereof are the ways of death.*[9] Genesis 3:1 tells us that the serpent was subtle – shrewd and cunning – he made it "seem right" to partake of the forbidden fruit.

Disobedience to God's commandments and disagreement with His Covenant always result in the "ways of death." The prefix "dis," as in dis-obedience and dis-agreement, means opposite of or apart from. The "ways of death" that occur when

31

we dis-obey God include dis-ease, dis-order, dis-tress (tress comes from the Latin word "tresse" - braid, hence distress means unraveled), and dis-aster (aster is Latin for star, so disaster implies a dis-ruption in the order of the universe).

Although they had been granted a significant degree of light, the people of Sodom and Gomorrah did not have God's written law. The Hebrew Torah contains God's written terms of the Abrahamic Covenant, which He gave to the children of Israel four hundred years later. The Ten Commandments, written on tablets of stone, were given through Moses to make plain to the people what He had already *"written in their hearts"* (their conscience). [10]

Moreover, all of the writings of the Old Testament, including the wisdom and poetry of the Prophets, the Psalms and Proverbs provide spiritual enlightenment:

> The entrance of Your Word gives light; it gives understanding to the simple. (Psalm 119:130)

> The commandment is a lamp, and the law a light; reproofs of instruction are the way of life. (Proverbs 6:23)

God's light clearly revealed through His written Word is superior in degree to the light of conscience and the light of creation. Furthermore, God's written law shines a bright light on our sinfulness so that we will recognize our need for a Savior. The Apostle Paul said, *"by the law is the knowledge of sin."* [11] He further explained, *"the law was our tutor to bring us to Christ, that we might be justified by faith."*[12]

The Light of Covenant

The disobedience of Adam and Eve is known as "the fall of man." After the fall, God began His pursuit to reconcile man with himself through different kinds of Covenants (agreements). Since God is perfectly just, the only way for God to restore man's relationship with Him was to provide a substitute to pay the death penalty for man's transgression. God accepted the sacrificial death of animals as a temporary substitute and a way of "covering" man's sin until He could ultimately send His Son to pay the full penalty. The Law says that without the shedding of blood there is no remission for sin.[13]

In the church I was raised in, we didn't study the Bible in Sunday school, and I didn't come to know the Lord until I was a teenager, so when I began reading the Bible, it made sense to me to start in the New Testament. I was doing a lot of babysitting at the time, so after I got the kids to bed, I would spend hours reading my paper back New Testament. It was a 1973 edition of the Living Bible, called "The Way." When I went to Bible College after high school, I still had not read through the Old Testament. In one of my courses, Old Testament Survey, the instructor would often say, "You remember when Moses..." or "You remember when Samuel..." I decided I had better start reading the Bible from the beginning!

As I started to read The Book of Genesis, I came to the part in chapter four where Cain and Abel both brought offerings to God. Cain was a farmer and brought fruit from the ground and Abel was a shepherd and brought the firstborn of his flock. It didn't seem fair to me that God respected Abel's offering but didn't have respect for Cain's, so I decided to ask my roommate about the story. (She had been a Christian a lot longer than I had.) As I got up from the kitchen table in my apartment where I was reading, I suddenly felt the Holy Spirit nudge me and say, "Why don't you ask me?" I sat back down in anticipation of learning something new.

What I learned, I will never forget. I wrote this in the margin of my Bible: Abel recognized that his sin deserved death. His lamb was a substitute.

The Old Testament (Old Covenant) included numerous written laws and involved multiple animal sacrifices - neither was able to do away with sin or change man's sinful nature. But in the New Testament (New Covenant), John the Baptist pointed to Jesus and exclaimed, *"Behold! The Lamb of God who takes away the sin of the world!" (John 1:29)*

The Light of Christ

Finally, the greatest light-source available to mankind in this present world is *"the light of the glorious gospel of Christ"* *(2 Corinthians 4:4)*. The Book of Hebrews compares and contrasts the Old Covenant with the New Covenant, demonstrating the Old Covenant's fulfillment in the person and work of Jesus Christ. The Epistle to the Hebrews magnifies this new and greater Covenant, which was established upon better promises. The introduction to Hebrews presents an awesome description of Christ as the ultimate Light:

In many separate revelations [each of which set forth a portion of the Truth] and in different ways God spoke of old to [our] forefathers in and by the prophets, [But] in the last of these days He has spoken to us in [the person of a] Son, Whom He appointed Heir and lawful Owner of all things, also by and through Whom He created the worlds and the reaches of space and the ages of time [He made, produced, built, operated, and arranged them in order]. He is the sole expression of the glory of God [the Light-being, the out-raying or radiance of the divine], and He is the perfect imprint and very image of [God's] nature, upholding and maintaining and guiding and propelling the universe by His mighty word of power. When He had by offering Himself accomplished our cleansing of sins and riddance of guilt, He sat down at the right hand of the divine Majesty on high. (Hebrews 1:1-3 Amplified)

My Testimony

I came to "The Light" in October of 1975. I was born again while attending a weekend Bible Camp retreat. My parents were planning to go up to their place in Minnesota that weekend, but I didn't want to miss the Homecoming football game and all the festivities that surrounded it. I asked a friend of mine if I could spend the weekend with her. She let me know she would be missing Homecoming too because she was going to a Bible Camp retreat, but she welcomed me to go with her. I told her, "If we're going to miss the football game, let's miss it to go 'up north!' It's beautiful up there! You can come with me to Minnesota instead!" She insisted she would not miss her retreat. That aroused my curiosity enough to want to check it out. I wondered how a Bible Camp retreat could be better than the Homecoming game!

I grew up believing in God and attending church, but I do not remember ever hearing the gospel until that weekend. My friend told me to bring a Bible, so I dusted off the one I had been presented in Sunday school a few years before, but had never read. Some of the pages were still stuck together.

The reason I had not read it was because when Bibles were given to our class as a gift from the pastor of my church, The First Congregational United Church of Christ, the teacher had us play the "telephone game" to illustrate how the Bible was written. She whispered a story into the ear of one of the girls in my class. The room was noisy and she didn't catch everything that was said, but she wasn't allowed to ask any questions or have the teacher repeat the story. She was told to whisper the same story into someone else's ear. This process was repeated until the last person in the class heard "the story." This person told the story out loud. Everyone laughed because it didn't match the one they heard. Then the teacher told us that this is how the Bible was written. By the time the stories were written down, they were much different than how they really happened. Why would I be interested in reading the Bible if it couldn't be trusted?

When I was almost 40 years old, I met up with another friend from my hometown who grew up attending the same church I was raised in. We went to Sunday school together as well as junior high and high school. I hadn't seen her for many years. She was married with children and still a member of that church. She asked me, "How in the world did you ever decide to become a minister?"

I began by reminding her of the Bibles with the red leather covers we were presented in Sunday school as kids, and the misleading "telephone game" we played, which discouraged me from reading mine. She questioned, "So that is not how the Bible was written?" I responded, "Some of the stories in the Bible were told orally before they were written, but all Scripture was given by inspiration of God."[14] I shared with her the facts about the canonization and preservation of the Scriptures as well as my testimony of coming to Christ and being called into the ministry.

The next day she made a point to contact me. She said, "I have to tell you something. I couldn't sleep last night after our conversation yesterday. I am a Sunday school teacher now and I have been teaching the kids the same thing we were taught about how the Bible was written, playing the same game we learned to illustrate it. I kept thinking about the kids in my class that may have been discouraged from reading the Bible or may have even turned away from God because of something I said!"

I was humbled by her honesty. I reassured her that God still used that Bible, given to me by her church (our church at the time), to speak to me at the Bible Camp retreat where I came to know Christ.

The minister at the Camp preached from the Book of Romans, opening his message with chapter three: *"None are righteous, no not one. For all have sinned and fall short of the glory of God." (Romans 3:10, 23)* He illustrated this truth by describing sheep trying to jump over a fence, all of them *"falling short."* I had always reasoned that if I didn't murder any one or do anything *really* bad I would make it to heaven, but my conscience told me something was wrong. When I would lay my head on my pillow at night, even after saying my prayers, I did not have a "blessed assurance." The words in these verses seemed to jump right off the page of that red leather Bible and speak directly to my heart.

I asked the friend who brought me, "What are we going to do then?" She said, "Keep listening." That put me on the edge of my seat. He proceeded on the "Roman's Road": *"For the wages of sin is death,"*[15] illustrating wages as something we deserve, something we have earned. *"But the gift of God is eternal life in Christ Jesus our Lord."*[16] A gift is not something we earn or deserve.

The minister went on to explain how God made a way for us to be saved: *"But God demonstrates His own love toward us, in that while we were still sinners, Christ died for us."*[17] Jesus died on the cross bearing the penalty we deserved so that we could receive eternal life as a gift. He concluded with this bible verse: *"If you confess with your mouth the Lord Jesus and believe in your heart that God has raised Him from the dead, you will be saved."*[18]

The minister invited those who wanted to be saved to get out of their seats and come to the front for prayer. I asked my friend if I should go. She said, "No, you don't have to." But when I got back to our cabin and climbed up on my bunk, I couldn't go to sleep until I prayed. I wanted to make sure I would go to heaven when I died. I told God that I believed what I heard that night; I believed Jesus died for my sins. Then I remembered when I was a little kid attending vacation Bible School with my cousin, I heard about asking Jesus to come into my heart. So sitting there in the dark on that cabin bunk bed, I prayed, "Jesus, I believe in you! Come into my heart and live forever!"

The next day the sky was a more beautiful blue than I had ever seen before; the grass was a richer green than I'd ever noticed before; the cool breeze blowing through the autumn leaves on the trees felt more wonderful than I had ever experienced before. The light of creation merged with the light of Christ. Suddenly I realized that I had come into contact with the One who created it all!

Later I heard the song, "*He's Everything to Me.*" I cried. The lyrics were my testimony exactly.

He's Everything to Me

In the stars His handiwork I see
On the wind He speaks with majesty
Tho' He ruleth over land and sea
What is that to me?

I will celebrate nativity
For it has a place in history
Sure He came to set His people free
But what is that to me?

'Til by faith I met Him face to face
And I felt the wonder of His grace
Then I knew that He was more
Than just a God who didn't care
Who lived away out there
And now He walks beside me day by day
Ever watching o're me lest I stray
Helping me to find that narrow way
He's everything to me[19]

If we are going to take seriously the warning of Sodom, as the Scriptures clearly admonish us to, we must ask ourselves: How much light have we been granted (first, as individuals; then, as Americans)? And how are we responding to that light?

Rejection of light is a serious matter!

Chapter 3
When Judgment Comes

In the tenth chapter of the Book of Matthew, we read about Jesus choosing His twelve disciples and commissioning them to go and preach the gospel to *"the lost sheep of the house of Israel."*[1] Promising to confirm their message with accompanying signs, He gave them power to heal the sick, cleanse the lepers, raise the dead, and cast out demons.[2] He then assigns this shuddering indictment upon individuals and cities that reject their message:

> And whoever will not receive you nor hear your words, when you depart from that house or city, shake off the dust from your feet. Assuredly, I say to you, it will be more tolerable for the land of Sodom and Gomorrah in the day of judgment than for that city! (Matthew 10:14-15)

In the next chapter of Matthew, Jesus similarly rebukes the city of Capernaum. Located on the northern shore of the Sea of Galilee, Capernaum was a prosperous fishing village, fruitful agricultural region, and busy trading center - a thriving metropolis for its day. Jesus selected this city to be the base of His public ministry after leaving His hometown of Nazareth.

> And leaving Nazareth, He came and dwelt in
> Capernaum, which is by the sea, in the regions
> of Zebulun and Naphtali, that it might be ful-
> filled which was spoken by Isaiah the prophet,
> saying:"The land of Zebulun and the land of
> Naphtali, By the way of the sea, beyond the
> Jordan, Galilee of the Gentiles: The people who
> sat in darkness have seen a great light,
> And upon those who sat in the region and shad-
> ow of death Light has dawned.
> (Matthew 4:13-16)

Many miracles were performed here, including the healing of the paralytic lowered through the roof to reach Jesus, the
healing of the centurion's servant afflicted with palsy, and the
raising of Jairus' daughter from the dead.

This is what Jesus predicted concerning Capernaum:

> And you, Capernaum, who are exalted to heav-
> en, will be brought down to Hades; for if the
> mighty works which were done in you had been
> done in Sodom, it would have remained until this
> day. But I say to you that it shall be more tolera-
> ble for the land of Sodom in the day of judgment
> than for you. (Matthew 11:23-24)

I have visited Capernaum, "The Hometown of Jesus,"

several times while touring Israel. Archaeological excavations have revealed the ancient synagogue where Jesus taught, as well as the nearby house where Jesus healed Peter's mother-in-law of a fever. As Jesus predicted, the city was reduced to ruins. It is now a popular tourist site in the Holy Land.

Jesus said that if the people of Sodom and Gomorrah had been afforded the same opportunity to hear the gospel and witness the miracles that the people of Capernaum witnessed, they would have repented, and the city of Sodom would still be there! As terrible as the sin and subsequent destruction of Sodom and Gomorrah were, He said their future judgment would be more tolerable than that of Capernaum.

According to Jesus, judgment is relative to the degree of light granted. This is true regarding individuals; it is also true regarding cities, states, and nations.

When King Chederlaomer and his allied armies attacked Sodom, the people of Sodom were given a warning - relatively speaking, this was a mini-judgment. This was their wake up call! But this warning was ignored. When they had an encounter with Abraham and Melchizedek, God was granting them more light and more space to repent.

The Bible says God is *"longsuffering toward us, not willing that any should perish but that all should come to repentance."* *(2 Peter 3:9)* Approximately 17 more years passed before irreparable judgment came to Sodom. Even then, God sent angels to give them one last opportunity to escape.

Sodom or Salem? America, It's Your Choice

Angels Visit Lot

According to Genesis chapter 19, when two angels who appeared as men arrived into Sodom, Lot welcomed them as guests into his home and prepared a feast for them. Like his uncle Abraham, he recognized their godliness and treated them with honor.

> After the meal, as they were preparing to retire for the night, all the men of Sodom, young and old, came from all over the city and surrounded the house. They shouted to Lot, "Where are the men who came to spend the night with you? Bring them out so we can have sex with them." Lot stepped outside to talk to them, shutting the door behind him. "Please, my brothers," he begged, "don't do such a wicked thing."
> (Genesis 19:3–6 NLT)

Lot responded to the men's demand by calling their behavior *"wicked."* This angered the mob and they accused Lot of trying to be their judge and then tried to break down the door.[3] The angels protected Lot from their assault and struck the Sodomites with blindness. Losing their eyesight was their final warning, but it did not halt their lust - the men continued to grope for the door.[4]

According to the Apostle Peter's commentary in the New Testament, the behavior of the Sodomites at Lot's house was by no means the first time they had acted so wickedly. Peter said Lot's soul was tormented *"day after day"* by seeing and hearing their *"filthy conduct." (2 Peter 2:6-8)*

44

Likewise, the Book of Jude warns, *"And don't forget the cities of Sodom and Gomorrah and their neighboring towns, which were filled with sexual immorality and every kind of sexual perversion."* *(Jude 1:7 NLT)*

The angels urged Lot to warn as many of his relatives as he could and evacuate the city because destruction was imminent. The text says Lot's daughters' fiancés thought he was joking.[5] Early the next morning, Lot was still lingering. The angels rushed Lot and his family, taking them by their hands and leading them out of the city. The angels warned, *"Escape for your life! Do not look behind you nor stay anywhere in the plain. Escape to the mountains, lest you be destroyed."* *(Genesis 19:17)*

> Then the LORD rained brimstone and fire on Sodom and Gomorrah, from the LORD out of the heavens. So He overthrew those cities, all the plain, all the inhabitants of the cities, and what grew on the ground. But his wife looked back behind him, and she became a pillar of salt. (Genesis 19:24–26)

Astronomical Evidence

In chapter two I quoted Dr. George Adam Smith's commentary about the destruction of Sodom and Gomorrah. He pointed out that the glare of this catastrophe "is flung down the whole length of Scriptural history." In the Archeological Supplement section of my Thompson Chain Reference Bible, however, he said, "the ruins it left have disappeared."

Dr. Smith died in 1942. More than likely, he was aware of the ancient clay disk found at the site of Nineveh, about 600 miles east of Sodom in the mid-19th century by archeologist Henry Layard. Scientists have attempted to unravel its mystery for the past 150 years. But only recent technological advancement has allowed the cuneiform symbols on this ancient tablet to be deciphered.

In 2008, several news outlets reported on the decoding of this artifact and a documentary regarding it was aired on the Science channel. Known as the "Planisphere" in the British museum where it has been displayed, this clay tablet was apparently used by an ancient Sumerian astrologer to record a very sophisticated interpretation of the night sky thousands of years ago. A number of identifiable constellations, and what appeared to be an enormous asteroid moving across the sky, were part of the recorded data.

Using modern software with computer modeling to recreate the ancient night sky, rocket scientists Alan Bond and Mark Hempsell painstakingly searched for months until they were able to pinpoint the sightings described on the disk to a date, with an exact match of the night sky: shortly before dawn on June 29 in the year 3123 BC.

The trajectory of the asteroid put the impact site, not in Israel, but in Kofels, Austria, where an asteroid hit has been suspected for many years as evidenced by a giant landslide. But a crater has never been found. However, because of the low angle of the asteroid's trajectory – around six degrees – the scientists determined an airburst was more likely. They suspect the asteroid clipped a mountain, causing it to explode and turning it into a fireball as it travelled down the valley, and no longer a solid object when it hit Kofels. The mega-ton blast would have created a plume of billions of tons of debris (fire and brimstone) over the Dead Sea area (Sodom and Gomorrah) with estimated ground temperatures of 400 degrees Fahrenheit. A mushroom cloud of smoke would have been seen for hundreds of miles the following morning.

> And Abraham went early in the morning to the place where he had stood before the LORD. Then he looked toward Sodom and Gomorrah, and toward all the land of the plain; and he saw, and behold, the smoke of the land which went up like the smoke of a furnace. (Genesis 19:27–28)

The asteroid, as witnessed and recorded on the Planisphere, was 1¼ kilometers in diameter (3/4 mile). The impact of an asteroid this size would be equivalent to more than 1,000 tons of TNT – 100 times more powerful than the world's largest nuclear weapon. The allied bombings of Hamburg during World War 2 were codenamed "Operation Gomorrah" because of the devastating firestorm effect of the campaign of the air raids, which killed over 40,000 people. The atomic bombs used on the cities of Hiroshima and Nagasaki during the final stage of World War 2, which killed at least 129,000 people, were described by President Harry Truman, when calling for Japan's surrender, as "a rain of ruin from the air, the like of which has never been seen on earth."[6] But according to the Bible, and according to the astronomical evidence discovered on the Sumerian Planisphere, such a "rain of ruin from the air" *was seen* on earth once before![7]

Geological Evidence

This year, our church had the honor of hosting Las Vegas' seventh "*A Night to Honor Israel.*" My husband David has served voluntarily as the Nevada State Director of Christians United for Israel (CUFI) under the leadership of the founder and president, John Hagee, since its inception in 2006, and currently serves as Regional Director. CUFI is now the largest pro-Israel organization in the United States with a membership that exceeds three million as of this year. (Our involvement with CUFI is one of the ways we are "choosing Salem!")

"*A Night to Honor Israel*" is a non-partisan celebration and unconditional tribute to the State of Israel and the Jewish people. The generous offerings received at these events have enabled CUFI Nevada to support several worthy causes in Israel including CELEB, which serves home-bound Holocaust survivors, and the Orly Absorption Center in Arad, which helps Ethiopian Jews returning to Israel adjust to Israeli culture.

Since 2012 David and I have had the privilege of hosting CUFI sponsored "Pastors Familiarization Tours" to Israel - taking pastors of various denominations from our region who have never been to the Holy Land. They travel there as "tourists" but many return as "Zionists," advocating for Israel.

One of the fascinating sites we visit on our tours is Masada - the ancient fortress of Herod the Great, which was built on top of an isolated plateau, overlooking the area of the Dead Sea. Located in southern Israel, and bordering Jordan, the Dead Sea is the lowest place on earth - its shores are 1,388 ft. below sea level. The "cities of the plain" were once located in this valley, then "*well watered everywhere (before the Lord destroyed Sodom and Gomorrah) like the garden of the Lord*" *(Genesis 13:10)*. From the top of Masada, the view is now barren desert for as far as the eye can see.

Regional climate collapse from the WW2 bombings in Hamburg, Hiroshima, and Nagasaki was predicted to effect the vegetation for up to forty years after the war, but restoration came after only a few years. On the other hand, climate collapse from the destruction of Sodom and Gomorrah has affected the vegetation in the region of the "cities of the plain" until this day.

The hyper-saline waters of the Dead Sea (eight times saltier than the ocean) prevent fish and aquatic plants from living in it. Tourists have fun taking pictures of each other floating without assistance while reading a newspaper. An unusual feature is its constant discharge of asphalt - small black pebbles of bitumen from deep seeps constantly being spit up.[8]

Another extraordinary geological phenomenon is a mountain of crystalline salt, five miles long and 300 feet high, along the southwestern shore of the Dead Sea, named Jebel Usdum, Arabic for "Mount Sodom." One of the pillars on the top of this formation is known as "Lot's wife."[9]

Archeological Evidence

The Madaba Mosaic Map is an intricate and unique piece of art that was discovered in 1897 under the ruins of a Byzantine church built in the 6th century AD in the ancient town of Madaba (in Jordan). It is the oldest known geographical floor mosaic map in art history, covering the area of the Holy Land from Lebanon to the Nile Delta and from the Mediterranean Sea to the Eastern Desert, including a detailed image of Jerusalem. Since Israel's recapturing of Jerusalem during the Six Day War in 1967, archeological excavations have continued to substantiate the map's accuracy. For example, in 2010, large paving stones were discovered, which confirmed the map's depiction of a wide central street through the center of the Old City.

One of the towns named on the Madaba Mosaic Map, located near the Dead Sea, is Zoar (the smallest of the ancient "cities of the plain" and the one God spared per Lot's request). Following the map to Zoar, archeologists came to a village still thriving, called Soffie, where the ruins of another Byzantine church were discovered. This seventh century church was built around a cave from the Early Bronze Age and Middle Bronze Age. An inscription was found in the mosaics of the church: "Sanctuary of St. Lot."

> "But I cannot go to the mountains. Disaster would catch up to me there, and I would soon die. See, there is a small village nearby. Please let me go there instead; don't you see how small it is? Then my life will be saved." "All right," the angel said, "I will grant your request. I will not destroy that little village. But hurry! For I can do nothing until you are there." From that time on, that village was known as Zoar. (Genesis 19:19-22 NLT)

The Warning of the Prophets

In the Old Testament, God often used His prophets to warn the nation of Israel of the consequences of forsaking the Covenant He made with them. Sometimes they would even compare Israel's sins to the sins of Sodom and Gomorrah. The Book of the Prophet Isaiah begins with a terrible indictment, calling the nation's leaders *"rulers of Sodom." (Isaiah 1:10)*

Isaiah bewails Israel's wickedness:

Hear, O heavens, and give ear, O earth! For the LORD has spoken: "I have nourished and brought up children, And they have rebelled against Me; The ox knows its owner And the donkey its master's crib; But Israel does not know, My people do not consider." Alas, sinful nation, A people laden with iniquity, A brood of evildoers, Children who are corrupters! They have forsaken the LORD, They have provoked to anger The Holy One of Israel, They have turned away backward.... Unless the LORD of hosts Had left to us a very small remnant, We would have become like Sodom, We would have been made like Gomorrah. (Isaiah 1:2–4, 9)

Like the Bible as a whole, the 66 chapters in The Book of Isaiah are laced with a redemptive theme. For example, in chapter 53, Isaiah prophesied concerning the coming Messiah with a profound description of Him willingly offering Himself up *"as a lamb to the slaughter,"* suffering the wrath of God for our sins. But in chapter three, Isaiah points out a startling similarity between Israel's behavior and that of Sodom's.

The look on their countenance witnesses against them, And they declare their sin as Sodom; They do not hide it. Woe to their soul! For they have brought evil upon themselves. (Isaiah 3:9)

The New Living Translation renders it like this: *"They sin openly like the people of Sodom. They are not one bit ashamed."* The Message Bible says, *"Brazen in their depravity, they flout their sins like degenerate Sodom."* And the New International Version says, *"They parade their sin like Sodom; they do not hide it."*

Jeremiah laments over the sins of the spiritual leaders, holding them responsible for the nation's lack of repentance:

> Also I have seen a horrible thing in the prophets of Jerusalem: They commit adultery and walk in lies; They also strengthen the hands of evildoers, So that no one turns back from his wickedness. All of them are like Sodom to Me, And her inhabitants like Gomorrah. (Jeremiah 23:14)

Ezekiel calls Sodom Israel's "sister":

> Behold, this was the iniquity of your sister Sodom: pride, overabundance of food, prosperous ease, and idleness were hers and her daughters'; neither did she strengthen the hand of the poor and needy. And they were haughty and committed abominable offenses before Me; therefore I removed them when I saw it and I saw fit. (Ezekiel 16:49-50 Amplified)

Ezekiel names some of the sins of Sodom, putting pride at the top of the list. Sodom was a prosperous city. Instead of acknowledging God and thanking Him for their blessings, the people became proud, idle, and selfish. In their haughtiness they "committed abominable offenses" before the Lord.

These prophetic rebukes, comparing Israel with Sodom, were intended to wake up the nation!

Chapter 4
America's Beginnings

Christopher Columbus (whose name means Christ-bearer), took off from a harbor in Spain in 1492 to "sail the ocean blue." The first great American historian, George Bancroft (1800-1891), assessed his voyage as "the most memorable maritime enterprise in the history of the world." Indeed, he opened up the New World to the Old. Many people today, however, do not know that Columbus was motivated by his Christian faith to carry the light of the gospel to dark and distant lands. Furthermore, he wanted to reach the West Indies to open up a new trade route and raise money for his ultimate goal of recapturing Jerusalem (Salem) from the Muslims.

In his Book of Prophecies, a volume he penned in 1505, Columbus wrote:

> It was the Lord who put into my mind (I could feel His hand upon me) to sail to the Indies. All who heard of my plan rejected it with laughter, ridiculing me. There is no question that the inspiration was from the Holy Spirit, because He comforted me with rays of marvelous illumination from the Holy Scriptures.[1]

Sodom or Salem? America, It's Your Choice

He further wrote:

> For the execution of the Indies I did not make use
> of intelligence, mathematics, or maps. It is simply
> the fulfillment of what Isaiah prophesied...These
> are great and wonderful things for the earth, and
> the signs are that the Lord is hastening the end.
> The fact the gospel must still be preached to so
> many lands in such a short time – this is what
> convinces me.[2]

The following is the prayer he and his crew prayed daily
on their long and difficult voyage:

> Blessed be the light of day
> And the Holy Cross, we say:
> And the Lord of Verity
> And the Holy Trinity.
> Blessed be th' immortal soul
> And the Lord who keeps it whole
> Blessed be the light of day
> And He who sends the night away.[3]

Christopher Columbus named the first island on which
they landed "San Salvador" meaning Holy Savior. Other lands
he named include "Trinidad" (Trinity) and "Vera Cruz" (True
Cross). In describing his discovery of America to King Ferdi-
nand of Spain, Columbus wrote:

Therefore let the king and queen, the princes
and their most fortunate kingdoms, and all other
countries of Christendom give thanks to our Lord
and Savior Jesus Christ, who bestowed upon us
so great a victory and gift. Let religious proces-
sions be solemnized; let sacred festivals be giv-
en; let the churches be covered with festive gar-
lands. Let Christ rejoice on earth, as he rejoices
in heaven, when he foresees coming to salvation
so many souls of people hitherto lost.[4]

Tragically, many Europeans who followed Columbus to
the New World mistreated and exploited the Native Americans.
However, we must beware of the revisionist political movement
attempting to defame Columbus and remake America into an entirely secular society. Christopher Columbus Day is seldom even
mentioned in public schools anymore, much less celebrated.

The Pledge of Allegiance was written to commemorate
the 400th anniversary of Columbus' voyage. President Dwight
D. Eisenhower, who signed into law the Pledge, including the
phrase "under God," said:

Without God, there could be no American form
of Government, nor an American way of life.
Recognition of the Supreme Being is the first
– the most basic – expression of Americanism.
Thus the founding fathers of America saw it, and
thus with God's help, it will continue to be.[5]

Sodom or Salem? America, It's Your Choice

The Protestant Reformation

During the century that followed the discovery of the New World, Roman Catholic colonization of much of South and Central America occurred; however, God preserved "the land of the free and the home of the brave" for a people He had yet to prepare through the Protestant Reformation in Europe. God used the invention of the printing press and men like Martin Luther and John Calvin to restore to the human race what the Dark Ages had stolen from them: personal faith in the infallible Word of God, instead of the word of a pope, priest, or king. Thousands of protestant believers were burned at the stake for proclaiming the authority of the Scriptures over corrupt papal authority. The illumination of the Scriptures brought about the individual and inward liberty necessary to resist religious tyranny and prepare the way for the establishment of "a government of the people, by the people, and for the people."

John Wycliffe has been called the "Morning Star of the Reformation" because the first rays of light from the Dark Ages began to shine forth when he translated the entire Bible from Latin into English for the first time in the 14th Century. Wycliffe believed that "Scripture must become the common property of all." Similarly, during the 15th Century, one of God's chief instruments in England was William Tyndale. Tyndale spent most of his life fulfilling his vision of getting the Scriptures translated into English and available to the common man. In 1536, he was betrayed, arrested, strangled, and burned at the stake as a heretic, but he faithfully prayed for his persecutors, specifically for King Henry VIII, who, after Tyndale's death, authorized the sale and reading of the Bible throughout the kingdom. Henry and England split from the Roman Catholic Church and set up the Church of England. Although Henry was not a godly man, God used him and these events for the advancement of religious and civil liberties. As the people began embracing the Word of God for themselves, a divine fire consumed their hearts and both the "Puritan" movement and the "Separatist" movements were birthed in England.

Pilgrims and Puritans

The Pilgrims, called "Separatists" because they refused to conform to the heretical practices of the Church of England, first fled to Holland to escape persecution, and from there, made their voyage to America. Part of their purpose in coming to America was to give their children a proper education and to protect them from the ungodly influences of the more secularized culture of Holland.

The Pilgrims had intended to land in Virginia where there was already some form of governmental jurisdiction, but as fate would have it, they were blown off course and landed at Plymouth Rock. While still aboard the ship, they decided to do something that would prove to change the course of history: they drafted The Mayflower Compact "in the name of God." America's first self-governing document was the Mayflower Compact. It became the cornerstone for our present Constitution. Historian Paul Johnson, in his book entitled *A History of the American People*, writes of the importance of this document:

> It is an amazing document.... What was remarkable about this particular contract was that it was not between a servant and a master, or a people and a king, but between a group of like-minded individuals and each other, with God as a witness and symbolic co-signatory.[6]

These God-fearing adventurers of 1620 desired so strongly to base their civic lives together on the laws of God that, in spite of their long tumultuous journey, they refused to get off the ship and set foot on their new homeland until they had first drafted and signed this covenant. Peter Marshall, co-author of the classic book, *The Light and the Glory*, offers this observation:

> This was the only place on the face of the earth where free Christian people were creating their own government, electing their own civil leadership – the only time in history, as a matter of fact, when a nation, from scratch, was based on God's Word.[7]

Nearly a decade later, the Puritans (also dissenting English Protestants, but ones who sought to reform or "purify" the Church of England rather than "separate" from it), sailed to New England and created Bible-based commonwealths in order to practice a representative form of government. These commonwealths also paved the way for the United States Constitution, which governs us today. As I was researching for this book, I was amazed to be reminded that the first Puritan settlement in the Massachusetts Bay colony in 1629 was named Salem.

Dr. David C. Gibbs, Jr., President of the Christian Law Association, suggested in his book, *One Nation Under God*: "The Puritans were trying to create a new Israel, a new theocracy where God was the ruler through the ministrations of elected magistrates."[8] There is no doubt that the original aim of these early settlers was to build a biblical "City on a Hill," a society established wholly on Biblical principles.

Rabbi Daniel Lapin, an Orthodox Jewish Rabbi, in his book, *America's Real War*, points out the deep and endless similarities between the birth of ancient Israel and the founding of America. Both nations were founded on an ideal born in the hearts of the people. He said that at almost every step, America was led by men who "acted Jewish": "To both Israel's and America's founders, the Bible was as vital for the safe operation of human society as any manufacturer's instruction manual would be for the safe operation of a complex piece of machinery."[9]

Early Education

For the first 200 years in America, all education was based upon a Christian worldview, with the Bible as the primary textbook. The New England Primer, introduced in Boston in 1690, was the first textbook to be printed and used to instruct colonial children. The book included The Lord's Prayer and the Apostle's creed, as well as many hymns and prayers. Here is how the book, used for more than a century, taught children the alphabet:

A

In Adam's fall
We sinned all.

B

Heaven to find;
The Bible Mind.

C

Christ crucify'd
For sinners dy'd[10]

Harvard, America's first college, was founded in 1636 and named after the Reverend John Harvard whose monetary donations helped construct some of the school buildings and whose donated books founded the library (the oldest library in the United States). Many of our founding fathers were trained at Harvard, including signers of the Declaration of Independence such as John Adams and John Hancock. Established as a school to train ministers of the Gospel, the educational philosophy of Harvard was literally "written in stone" and one can still find these words etched in old English:

> After God had carried us safe to New-England, and we had built our houses, provided necessaries for our livelihood, reared convenient places for Gods worship, and settled the civil government, one of the next things we longed for, and

looked after was to advance learning and perpetuate it to posterity; dreading to leave an illiterate ministry to the churches, when our present ministers shall lie in the dust.[11]

Harvard further admonished:

> Let every student be plainly instructed and ... consider well the main end of his life and studies is to know God and Jesus Christ which is eternal life (John 17:3) and therefore to lay Christ in the bottom as the only foundation of all sound knowledge and learning.[12]

Other early American universities, such as Yale, Princeton, and Columbia, which produced our early American leaders, had similar mottoes and stated purposes. For example, Yale admonished its students:

> Above all have an eye to the great end of all your studies, which is to obtain the clearest conceptions of Divine things and to lead you to a saving knowledge of God in his Son Jesus Christ.[13]

Princeton University President, John Witherspoon, also a signer of the Declaration of Independence and one who personally trained a number of African-American students at Princeton (unprecedented at that time in world history), instructed his students:

He is the best friend to American liberty, who is most sincere and active in promoting true and undefiled religion, and who sets himself with the greatest firmness to bear down profanity and immorality of every kind. Whoever is an avowed enemy of God, I scruple (hesitate) not to call him an enemy of his country.[14]

America's founders and early immigrants made tremendous sacrifices to leave the Old World where they had experienced harsh persecutions for their faith and witnessed civil atrocities under the banner of Christianity due to widespread Biblical illiteracy. They were convinced that if the common people could read and study the Scriptures for themselves, they would learn for themselves the limits God's Word puts on governing authorities and hence be equipped to resist government misbehavior. Therefore, America's first public education law, which required that schools be started in each community, was called "The Ole Deluder Satan Act." The law declared:

It being one chief project of that old deluder, Satan, to keep men from the knowledge of the Scriptures, as in former times by keeping them in an unknown tongue… so in these latter times by persuading from the use of tongues…It is therefore ordered that every township in this jurisdiction, after the Lord hath increased them to fifty households shall forthwith appoint one within their town to teach all such children…. [15]

This law, passed in 1647, was intended to defeat Satan, the "Old Deluder" who had, in times past, prevailed in keeping people ignorant of God's Word, which resulted in bad government and religious oppression.

The Great Awakening

By the 18th Century, in spite of British laws prohibiting the printing of English Bibles in America, there was hardly a free colonist in America who wasn't thoroughly schooled in the Scriptures. This did not mean, however, that the majority of Americans had a personal saving faith in Jesus Christ. In most of the colonies religion was enforced, and therefore had become cold and formal for many. But God sent the mighty wind of His Holy Spirit to the American wilderness, and through the preaching of evangelists such as Jonathan Edwards, a New Englander, and George Whitfield, an Englishman, what became known as "The Great Awakening" occurred from around 1730 to 1770.

Jonathan Edwards was one of colonial America's greatest intellects and foremost theologians. His messages emphasized the holiness of God, the depravity of man, and the necessity of personal salvation. He is best known for his famous sermon, "Sinners in the Hands of an Angry God."

George Whitfield was barred from the pulpits of England for preaching, "You must be born again," but during his seven trips to America he preached outside in open fields and effectively reached crowds of up to 20,000 people. Someone once asked him why he so often preached, "You must be born again." And he replied, "Because you *must* be born again!" Some of

Whitefield's most ardent followers were black slaves. The "Negro Spiritual," the beginning of what we now recognize as Black Gospel, and considered America's greatest contribution to the field of music, originated from the slaves during The Great Awakening.

The Great Awakening brought a movement of recognition of the sanctity of the life of every individual and encouraged numerous humanitarian efforts. Orphanages were started, effective missionary efforts began among the Native Americans as well as foreign lands, and many began to speak out against the evils of slavery.

Hundreds of thousands of conversions were reported as revival fires burned up and down the Eastern seaboard. The number of people in the churches more than doubled as whole towns came to Christ. Music and worship became an important part of colonial life, and hymns gained wide popularity, especially those written by Isaac Watts. Benjamin Franklin wrote in his *Autobiography*, "It was wonderful to see the change soon made in the manners of our inhabitants... one could not walk through the town in an evening without hearing psalms sung in different families of every street." [16]

Many historians agree that without the Great Awakening, there would have been no American Revolution. A key text for the Great Awakening also became a theme for the American Revolution: *"Behold, I make all things new." (Revelation 21:5)* The clergy of New England provided strength and inspiration, calling for godly resistance to British tyranny. Because of the color of their robes, these ministers became known as the "Black Regiment," some of them even conducted military drills after

Sunday services. The organized patriotic colonists were named "Minutemen" as they were ready to protect their towns from the British in a moment's notice. Dr. D. James Kennedy, in his outstanding book, *What if Jesus Had Never Been Born?* stated, "The road to American freedom was paved in large part by the pulpits of New England. Sermons from the colonial era helped to shape the American understanding that "resistance to tyranny is obedience to God." [17]

The Declaration of Independence

When in the Course of human events it becomes necessary for one people to dissolve the political bands which have connected them with another and to assume among the powers of the earth, the separate and equal station to which the Laws of Nature and of Nature's God entitle them, a decent respect to the opinions of mankind requires that they should declare the causes which impel them to the separation. We hold these truths to be self-evident, that all men are created equal, that they are endowed by their Creator with certain un-alienable Rights, that among these are Life, Liberty and the pursuit of Happiness. That to secure these rights, Governments are instituted among Men, deriving their just powers from the consent of the governed, — That whenever any Form of Government becomes destructive of these ends, it is the Right of the People to alter or to abolish it, and to institute new Government, laying its foundation on such principles and organizing its powers in such form, as to them shall seem most likely to effect their Safety and Happiness.[18]

The Declaration of Independence, penned by Thomas Jefferson, is our nation's "birth certificate." In the preamble, "the Laws of Nature and of Nature's God" are appealed to as our entitlement for separation. The 18th century phrase "laws of nature" was commonly understood to be God's universal laws written into creation. In fact, that term was used in the British law book of the day. "The second most often quoted source in the political writings of the American founding era (outside of the Bible) were the writings of Sir William Blackstone (1723-1780), a British jurist who wrote popular commentary on British common law." [19]

Blackstone expounds upon these terms, "the laws of Nature" and "of Nature's God" in a section of his *Commentaries* entitled, "Of the Nature of Laws in General":

Man, considered as a creature, must necessarily be subject to the laws of his creator, for he is entirely a dependent being... and consequently as man depends absolutely upon his Maker for everything, it is necessary that he should in all points conform to his Maker's will. This will of his Maker is called the Law of Nature.[20] This law of nature, being... dictated by God himself, is of course superior in obligation to any other. It is binding over all the globe in all countries, and at all times. No human laws are of any validity, if contrary to this; [21]

The second phrase, "and of Nature's God," was referring to Divine Law as revealed in the Holy Scriptures. This, too, is confirmed in Blackstone's Commentaries, as well as by other prominent Founding Fathers. For example, James Wilson, who was a leading legal theorist, one of the six original justices appointed by George Washington to the Supreme Court, and a signer of the Declaration and the Constitution, said:

> In compassion to the imperfection of our internal powers, our all gracious Creator, Preserver, and Ruler has been pleased to discover and enforce his laws by a revelation given to us immediately and directly from Himself. This revelation is contained in the Holy Scriptures. The moral precepts delivered in the sacred oracles form a part of the law of nature, are of the same origin and of the same obligation, operating universally and perpetually.... The law of nature and the law of revelation are both Divine: they flow, though in different channels, from the same adorable source. It is indeed preposterous to separate them from each other. The object of both is to discover the will of God and both are necessary for the accomplishment of that end. [22]

Thomas Jefferson spoke of "self-evident truths." In other words, he was saying there is no need to debate nor prove that man was created in the image of his Creator, and therefore, has rights that came from Him, not come from the State. These truths, he asserted, are "self-evident."

Among these God-given "inalienable Rights" are "Life, Liberty, and the Pursuit of Happiness." Our Declaration of Independence clearly states that citizens have a duty to require that their government recognize, secure, and protect these God-given rights.

Jefferson's final climactic words appealed to "the Supreme Judge of the World for the rectitude of our intentions," and he reinforced his appeal with this ending:

> And for the support of this Declaration, with a firm reliance on the protection of Divine Providence, we mutually pledge to each other our Lives, our Fortunes, and our sacred Honor. [23]

In essence, our Declaration of Independence was also *a declaration of dependence* upon Almighty God, the Supreme Judge of the World.

Chapter 5
We The People

We the people of the United States, in order to form a more perfect union, establish justice, insure domestic tranquility, provide for the common defense, promote the general welfare, and secure the blessings of liberty to ourselves and our posterity, do ordain and establish this Constitution for the United States of America.[1]
- The Preamble to the Constitution

The Declaration of Independence is America's birth certificate. The Constitution of the United States is what its name implies: it is our structure, our composition, and our system of beliefs and laws that constitute the core of who we are as a nation. Both of these founding documents enshrine our ideals of self-government and resistance to tyranny.

The Slime Pit of Slavery

While studying "The Battle of Four Kings Against Five" in Genesis chapter 13 (where I found the words Sodom and Salem), I discovered that the King of Sodom and the King of Gomorrah fell into slime pits as they were fleeing from enemy attacks. After the Holy Spirit pointed out to me that "we the people" are metaphorically the king of Sodom (meaning God is holding every U.S. citizen responsible for the wickedness in our nation because we are the ruling force in America just as the King Bera was the ruling force of Sodom), I began to notice several other analogies regarding America in the story. For example, I saw the slime pits as America's low points. Without a doubt, the most horrific "slime pit" in our nation's history was slavery, and one of our lowest points in our history was during our nation's Civil War.

The subject of slavery became an explosive issue following the Great Awakening and throughout the Revolutionary War. Some colonists, especially southern plantation owners, justified it as a "necessary evil." But the light of God's Word, and especially the light of the glorious Gospel of Christ, exposed it for what it really was – just plain evil. Slavery violated every principle of liberty for which the American patriots were fighting.

Some tried to justify it, but most of our founding fathers admitted that slavery was wrong and needed to be abolished. How to go about abolishing an institution that was so entrenched into society, and upon which the nation's economy had come to depend, was the complex question and problem to solve.

Among the most ardent and vocal opponents of slavery were Puritan ministers and revivalist preachers. Rev. Samuel Hopkins, a student of Jonathon Edwards, did a masterful job systematically dismantling all the arguments rationalizing slavery. Using the words of the Declaration of Independence "all men are created equal" and "endowed by their Creator with certain unalienable rights," he shrieked: "Oh, the shocking, the intolerable inconsistence!" He warned that for this sin "America is subject to divine justice."[2]

One of the delegates to the constitutional convention, a Christian statesmen from Virginia named George Mason, gave a similar stern warning:

> Every master of slaves is born a petty tyrant. They bring the judgment of heaven on a country. As nations cannot be rewarded or punished in the next world they must be in this. By an inevitable chain of causes & effects, providence punishes national sins by national calamities. [3]

By 1834, the anti-slavery movement had become well organized with one-third of its leaders being clergymen. The first anti-slavery convention stated:

> With entire confidence in the overruling justice of God, we plant ourselves upon the Declaration of Independence and the truths of divine revelation as upon the everlasting rock. We shall organize anti-slavery societies, if possible, in every city, town, and village in our land.[4]

These evangelical "abolition societies" eventually helped birth the Republican Party in 1854.

The Dred Scott Case

Dred Scott was a slave who had been taken by his owners to "free" states and territories in the 1830s, and later, with the moral and financial support of his abolitionist friends, sued for his freedom in a Missouri court. He lost his case in 1846 on a technicality, but in a new trial in 1850, a jury found in favor of Scott and his family. His owner, who was the widow of his previous owner, was not willing to accept the financial losses (a judge had ordered that wages for Scott be paid to and held in an account until the case was settled) and appealed to the Supreme Court of Missouri, which held that the Scotts were still legally slaves. In 1853, Dred Scott again sued his then current owner in federal court, and finally appealed to the Supreme Court of the United States.

On March 6, 1857, the Supreme Court's infamous ruling in the "Dred Scott Case" was handed down. In their landmark 7-2 decision, the Court held that "no Negro" (the term then used to describe anyone with African blood) "was or could ever be a citizen." Their decision invalidated the Missouri Compromise of 1820, which restricted slavery in U.S. Territories, thus declaring an Act of Congress to be unconstitutional.

The Supreme Court Was Wrong!

The Dred Scott decision proved to be a catalyst for the Civil War. Northern abolitionists were outraged and abolitionist ministers preached resistance to the decision. "If people obey this decision, they disobey God," they boldly asserted.

The Dred Scott ruling is unanimously denounced by scholars and politicians today, but at that time, many Democrats praised the ruling and characterized Republicans as lawless rebels - provoking disunion by their unwillingness to accept the Supreme Court's decision as the law of the land. Stephen A.

Douglas attacked the Republican position in the Lincoln-Douglas debates: "Mr. Lincoln goes for a warfare upon the Supreme Court of the United States, because of their judicial decision in the Dred Scott case. I yield obedience to the decisions in that court—to the final determination of the highest judicial tribunal known to our constitution."[5]

Abraham Lincoln unapologetically criticized the Supreme Court for its denial of the Law of God. Lincoln stated that if the Supreme Court's unconstitutional and ungodly ruling in the Dread Scott case were not overturned, "the people will have ceased to be their own rulers, having to that extent practically resigned their government into the hands of that eminent tribunal."[6] Abraham Lincoln's Second Inaugural Address is etched in stone at the Lincoln Memorial in Washington, D.C.:

> Fondly do we hope, fervently do we pray that this mighty scourge of war may speedily pass away. Yet, if God wills that it continue until all the wealth piled by the bondsman's two hundred and fifty years of unrequited toil shall be sunk, and until every drop of blood drawn with the lash shall be paid by another drawn with the sword, as was said three thousand years ago, so still it must be said, "the judgments of the Lord are true and righteous altogether."

Shortly before his assassination Lincoln wrote:

> On many a defeated field there was a voice louder

than the thundering of a cannon. It was the voice of God, crying, "Let my people go." We were all very slow in realizing it was God's voice, but after many humiliating defeats the nation came to believe it a great and solemn command. Great multitudes begged and prayed that I might answer God's voice by signing the Emancipation Proclamation, and I did it, believing we never should be successful in the great struggle unless the God of Battles has been on our side. [7]

By the courage of those who were enlightened by God's Word and willing to fight for what was right, we were rescued from the slime pit of slavery and our nation survived the Civil War. Following the Civil War there was a "new birth of freedom." In the greatest presidential speech in history, The Gettysburg Address (also etched in stone at the Lincoln Memorial), delivered at the gravesite of the soldiers, President Lincoln gave America the formula for a "new birth":

It is for us the living, rather, to be dedicated here to the unfinished work for which they who fought here have thus far so nobly advanced. It is rather for us to be here dedicated to the great task remaining before us that from these honored dead we take increased devotion to that cause for which they gave the last full measure of devotion -- that we here highly resolve that these dead shall not have died in vain, **that this nation, under God,**

**shall have a new birth of freedom and that
government of the people, by the people, for
the people, shall not perish from the earth.**[8]

The infamous "Dread Scott decision" by the Court, declaring blacks as property, was finally overturned by "we the
people" of the United States through a Constitutional Amendment - the 13th Amendment. The 14th Amendment was then proposed during the Reconstruction after the Civil War to guarantee
civil rights to the freed slaves. And the 15th Amendment ensured
their right to vote.

The Balance of Power

The separation of powers instituted in our Constitution
was based upon our Founding Father's Biblical understanding
of the sinfulness of man and his propensity toward evil. In craft-
ing the document that would provide the framework for self-
government and freedom, the Founders were careful to take into
consideration the temptation in human nature toward greed and
selfishness. James Madison said, "All men having power ought
to be distrusted." Benjamin Franklin echoed the same, "There is
scarce a king in a hundred who would not, if he could, follow
the example of Pharaoh, get first all the peoples' money, then
all their lands, and then make them and their children servants
forever." [9]

The concept of checks and balances withdrew from any
one man or group the ability to become tyrannical. The Constitution defines the function and the boundaries of each branch of

government.

> In a simple overview, Article I of the Constitu-
> tion sets forth the responsibilities of the Legis-
> lative branch, dedicating 109 lines to describing
> its powers; Article II addresses the duties of the
> Executive branch in 47 lines; and Article III has
> a mere 17 lines in its description of the responsi-
> bilities of the Judiciary. The fact that the Legisla-
> tive branch is listed first, coupled with the fact
> that nearly two-thirds of the lines describing the
> three branches of government are dedicated to
> the Congress, implies that our Founders believed
> it to be the most important and most powerful
> branch, with the Judiciary the least important and
> the least powerful.[12]

In addition to the separation of powers within the national government, our Founders held to the principle that most
powers should be decentralized among state and local governments with only a few necessary powers left to a national
government. This is what "federalism" is – "the distribution of
power between a central authority and the constituent units."[10]
The Constitution does not make the states administrative arms
of the federal government; rather, it secures state governments
with supreme authority over their areas of jurisdiction.

James Madison described this order when he said:

The powers delegated by the proposed Constitution to the federal government are few and defined. Those which are to remain in the State governments are numerous and indefinite.[11]

Moreover the 10th Amendment to the Constitution reads:

The powers not delegated to the United States by the Constitution, nor prohibited by it to the States, are reserved to the States respectively, or to the people.[12]

Thomas Jefferson also predicted the fate of veering from this federalist principle:

The true theory of our Constitution is surely the wisest and best ... (For) when all government ... shall be drawn to Washington as the centre of all power, it will render powerless the checks provided of one government on another, and wilt become as ... oppressive as the government from which we separated.[13]

All of our founding documents emphasize that laws and policies are to be established by "the consent of the governed," so it is logical that the Legislative branch was to be superior to the Judiciary, and that officials elected by the people to make laws would hold a more important position than unelected officials who interpret them. This did not mean the Judiciary was powerless. It was to provide a level of checks and balances on the other branches by reviewing the laws and judging them against the Constitution. This process is called "judicial review." In recent years, however, this term has been misleading and has wrongly turned into judicial activism, judicial revision, and even judicial tyranny. Long ago, Thomas Jefferson warned how this might occur:

> It has long, however, been my opinion, and I have never shrunk from its expression... that the germ of dissolution of our federal government is in the constitution of the federal Judiciary; ...working like gravity by night and by day, gaining a little today and a little tomorrow, and advancing its noiseless step like a thief, over the field of juris-diction, until all shall be usurped.[13] Taking from the States the moral rule of their citizens, and subordinating it to the general authority (federal government)... would... break up the foundations of the Union...[14]

Judicial Tyranny

History is to a country what memory is to an individual. When we forget who we are as a nation, we become confused and disoriented. This is what has happened to us over the past few decades. As a result of the memory loss of our true identity, we have bowed to judicial tyranny.

In the 1960s, after three centuries of prayer and Bible

reading in our schools, the Supreme Court struck down voluntary school prayer and ordered the removal of Bibles from public education. Following this decision, the number of crimes and the number of sexually transmitted diseases and teen pregnancies skyrocketed.

Following the moral vacuum of the 1960s, in an attempt to provide a solution to the epidemic of immorality and unwanted pregnancies, the High Court ruled in 1973 that unborn children are not persons and are not deserving of the protection of our Constitution and laws, thus unleashing the American holocaust.

In 1980, the U.S. Supreme Court ruled it was not permissible to post, or for school children to even see, The Ten Commandments, even though they are found in hundreds of government buildings and have been recognized for centuries as the basis for civil law in the Western World.

In 2003, after centuries of state laws prohibiting sodomy, the Supreme Court "discovered" a right to homosexual sodomy in our Constitution (perhaps in the same non-existent clause that guarantees women the right to abortion).

In 2013, the Supreme Court struck down the Defense of Marriage Act (DOMA), a federal law that passed both houses of Congress by large majorities and was signed into law by President Bill Clinton in 1996, whereby the federal government defined marriage as a legal union between one man and one woman, and whereby no state would be required to recognize as a marriage a same-sex relationship considered a marriage in another state.

Most recently, in 2015, the Supreme Court decided it could redefine the institution of marriage, an institution it did not create nor ordain.

The Supreme Court's Ruling on Same-Sex Marriage

The Supreme Court of the United States handed down their landmark 5-4 ruling in Obergefell v. Hodges on June 26, 2015, declaring that state laws banning same-sex marriage and state constitutions defining marriage as between a man and a woman are "unconstitutional." Ironically, they used the equal protection clause of the Fourteenth Amendment to base their opinion.[15] Chief Justice John Roberts wrote in his dissent that the Court's decision had "nothing to do with the Constitution," and Justice Antonin Scalia called it a "threat to American democracy."[16]

In his nine-page dissent, Justice Scalia compared the majority opinion to England's treatment of American colonies before the war of independence, stating that it perpetrated a more serious offence than the one that ignited the American Revolution. Indeed, "to allow the policy question of same-sex marriage to be considered and resolved by a select, patrician, highly unrepresentative panel of nine is to violate a principle even more fundamental than no taxation without representation: no social transformation without representation,"[17] he said.

Justice Scalia pointed out that not "a single evangelical Christian (a group that comprises about one quarter of Americans), or even a Protestant of any denomination" is to be found on the Court, which currently consists of six Catholics and three Jews. "Until the courts put a stop to it, public debate over same-sex marriage displayed American democracy at its best," Scalia asserted. But the Court's claim to "super-legislative power" bulldozed the right of the people to self-government, and a "system of government that makes the People subordinate to a committee of nine unelected lawyers does not deserve to be called a democracy."[18]

The most pungent and compelling statement in Justice Scalia's dissent in the Supreme Court's 5-4 majority ruling is this: "Today's decree says that my Ruler, and the Ruler of 320 million Americans coast-to-coast, is a majority of the nine lawyers on the Supreme Court."[19]

During the decade before the Supreme Court decision, the laws of 21 states banning same-sex marriage, and/or their state constitutions protecting the traditional definition of marriage, were struck down - not by the will of the people through legislation, but through the courts by federal judges. The Supreme Court's ruling disenfranchised the people of 13 more states.

Consider how quickly and how far we have removed ourselves from the Biblical principles from which our Constitution was framed. Even 20th century courts appealed to the Bible, like this one in 1963:

> Marriage was not originated by human law. When God created Eve, she was a wife to Adam; they then and there occupied the status of husband to wife and wife to husband... The truth is that civil government has grown out of marriage... which created homes, and population, and society, from which government became necessary... [Marriages] will produce a home and family that will contribute to good society, to free and just gov-

ernment, and to the support of Christianity... It would be sacrilegious to apply the designation "a civil contract" to such a marriage. It is that and more; a status ordained by God.[20]

How Did We Drift?

How did we drift so far from our Judeo-Christian heritage and values? The hard truth is, through ignorance and neglect, "we the people" have relinquished many of our individual and state's rights, and have allowed the federal government, especially the High Court, to ignore its Constitutional boundaries and assume powers the framers of the Constitution sought diligently to prevent.

In the parable found in Matthew 13:24-30, Jesus tells about the man who had planted a good field and woke up one day to find tares among his wheat. How did this happen? Jesus explained: While the good men were sleeping, an enemy came in and sowed the tares.

The principle of sowing and reaping in a nation is profoundly applicable when it comes to the education of our children. Abraham Lincoln said, "The philosophy of the classroom today will be the philosophy of government tomorrow."[21]

Many Christians in America have carelessly drifted off to sleep, removing themselves from active involvement in the political process, unknowingly surrendering their governmental influence and precious religious freedoms. Meanwhile, secular leaders have been elected, liberal secular judges appointed, and a secular humanist society has sprung up.

Several of our early U.S. Presidents were actively involved in Christian ministry. President Garfield was a minister of the Gospel. He warned Americans over a century ago:

> Now, more than ever before, the people are responsible for the character of their Congress. If that body be ignorant, reckless, and corrupt, it is because the people tolerate ignorance, recklessness, and corruption. If it be intelligent, brave, and pure, it is because the people demand these high qualities to represent them in the national legislature... If the next centennial does not find us a great nation... it will be because those who represent the enterprise, the culture, and the morality of the nation do not aid in controlling the political forces.[22]

Charles Finney, a prominent evangelist during America's Second Great Awakening in the early 1800s, admonished the church in his day:

> The Church must take the right ground in regard to politics...Politics are a part of religion in such a country as this, and Christians must do their duty to the country as part of their duty to God. God will bless or curse this nation according to the course Christians take in politics.[23]

Chapter 6
Wake Up! We're in a War!

Immediately following the September 11, 2001 terror attacks on our nation, President George W. Bush began to emphasize that our country was in "a different kind of war." Indeed, most of us had no idea we were in a war at all, but we suddenly realized that evil men had been plotting against us and we had been caught unaware and unprotected against an unthinkable assault. We now understand how unique and unconventional the war on terror is. Similarly, there is another war being waged in our nation that far too many of us are unaware of. The moral fabric of our country is unraveling, and the very foundations upon which our freedoms have been built are being compromised.

The Enemy Within

Robert H. Bork served as Solicitor General and Acting Attorney General of the United States. He wrote a *New York Times* bestselling book entitled: *Slouching Towards Gomorrah: Modern Liberalism and American Decline*. In the introduction, he addresses the dramatic decline in moral values and the current "cultural war" in the United States. Bork warned: "The distinctive features of Western civilization are in peril in ways not previously seen. This time the threat is not military... nor is it external... the enemy within us is modern liberalism."[1]

I read a cover story in *Charisma* magazine a few years ago by Robert Stearns entitled, *"Why Israel Matters."* In this article, Stearns offered this profound observation:

> Militant Islam is dedicated to global conquest and the destruction of Israel and America. Its adherents are daily sacrificing their children as homicide bombers to accomplish their aim. A spiritually complacent church seems unaware or in denial regarding **the twin threats** to the future of Western civilization—**radical Islam and secular humanism**.[2]

Robert Bork calls it *modern liberalism*; Robert Stearns calls it *secular humanism*. Both terms refer to an ideological enemy that is diametrically opposed to the Biblical worldview our founding fathers embraced and that helped to frame our constitution. Yet this is the ideology that is now predominate in our public schools, colleges and universities, and permeates Hollywood and the media. This "enemy within" is threatening to destroy our Judeo-Christian civilization.

While We Were Sleeping

There has arisen, from the secular humanistic society that sprung up "while we were sleeping," a sophisticated, well-funded campaign of deception, with a strategic marketing plan, to normalize and legitimize the "LGBT" (lesbian, gay, bisexual and transgendered) lifestyle and vilify those who oppose it. Make no mistake: the agenda of the "gay rights movement" goes way beyond protecting the civil rights of "LGBT Americans." Their expressed goal is *The Overhauling of Straight America.* Their plan, by this title, was published by *Guide Magazine* in 1987 and includes these objectives:

- Talk about gays and gayness as loudly and as often as possible.
- Portray gays as victims, not as aggressive challengers.
- Give protectors a just cause.
- Make gays look good.
- Make the victimizers look bad.[3]

Heralding the themes of "equality," "anti-discrimination," "civil rights," "diversity," and "fairness," groups such as the Human Rights Campaign, the National Lesbian and Gay Task Force, the Gay & Lesbian Alliance Against Defamation, and Lambda Legal have wielded their lobbying power and successfully convinced the courts, as well as other government entities, to sympathize and finally advocate for their agenda.

This was unmistakably the case in the repeal of the federal Defense of Marriage Act (DOMA). President Obama, in his Oath of Office, swore to defend the Constitution and our laws. The Department of Justice (DOJ) is responsible for the enforcement of the laws and the administration of justice in the United States. But after two years of persistent gay rights activism, including an open letter to the President from the Human Rights Campaign, Attorney General Eric Holder released a statement saying the President had instructed the DOJ not to defend the Defense of Marriage Act. In 2010, Edith Windsor, whose female partner died, filed a lawsuit against the federal government seeking a refund to her claim of federal estate tax exemptions for surviving spouses. After the 2013 Supreme Court's 5-4 ruling in favor of Windsor, dissenting Justice, Antonin Scalia, said that the majority opinion characterized opponents of same-sex marriage as "enemies of the human race."[4]

The Civil Rights Movement

Unlike the Gay Rights Movement, which began with the "Stonewall Riots" in the 1960's that erupted when police raided a gay bar in Manhattan after receiving complaints of gay men openly engaging in sodomy,[5] the Civil Rights Movement of the 1950s and 1960s, like the Abolitionist Movement a century earlier, was birthed out of the Church as Christians refused to remain silent in the face of evil.

The Abolitionist Movement of the 1800s ultimately pulled us out of the "slime pit" of slavery, but discrimination of Americans of African decent continued well into the next century. States continued to enact and enforce racial segregation laws, and the U.S. Supreme Court decided to uphold these laws in 1896 under the doctrine of "separate but equal." Finally, in 1954, the Supreme Court ruled in *Brown v. Board of Education of Topeka* that state laws that racially segregated public schools were unconstitutional according to the equal protection clause of the 14th Amendment, giving the Civil Rights Movement a momentous victory.

Dr. Martin Luther King, Jr., a Baptist minister, was the most notable of Christian leaders who resisted the cultural tide based upon his understanding that America's founding documents were not only on the right side of the Civil Rights cause, but most importantly, they were based upon Biblical truths. He helped organize non-violent protests and acts of civil disobedience, including the 1955 Montgomery Bus Boycott and the 1963 March on Washington, where he delivered his famous "I Have a Dream" speech.

One of the most courageous leaders and greatest orators in American History, Dr. King identified his source of inspiration in his *"Letter from a Birmingham Jail"*:

> We will win our freedom because the sacred heritage of our nation and the eternal will of God are embodied in our echoing demands.[6]

He addressed why he was compelled to break the law in order to change it:

> How does one determine whether a law is just or unjust? A just law is a man-made code that squares with the moral law or the law of God. An unjust law is a code that is out of harmony with the moral law.[7]

Of course, immorality and racism cannot be eradicated through legislation. But as hearts and lives are transformed by the power of the gospel, and Christians are awakened to their civic duties, their effect upon society should certainly include the enactment of laws that align with the law of God.

"We the People" and the law of God prevailed with the passing of the historical 1964 Civil Rights Act, which banned discrimination based on race, color, religion, sex, or national origin.

The Perversion

"Destruction is certain for those who say that evil is good and good is evil; that dark is light and light is dark." (Isaiah 5:20 NLT)

LGBT activist groups have successfully pressured the courts to perversely interpret the equality clause in the 14th Amendment, which was clearly intended to ensure former slaves "equal protection of the laws," to now apply not only to race and gender, which are immutable, but to "sexual orientation." These same activist groups are currently convincing federal agencies that the Civil Rights Act of 1964, which protects citizens against discrimination in public accommodations, public facilities, public education, and federally assisted programs, applies to "gender identity" (transgenders). The 1964 bill established the Equal Employment Opportunity Commission (EEOC). The EEOC has recently filed claims on behalf of transgender people under the Civil Rights Act in federal court. As I write, the Supreme Court has yet to hear such a case.

In 1972, an Education Amendment was passed, which, according to Title IX, prohibits discrimination on the basis of sex in educational institutions receiving federal aide. In 2010, the Office for Civil Rights of the U.S. Department of Education issued a letter of guidance regarding anti-bullying policies in schools, and in 2014, the Department "clarified" their guidance, noting: "Title IX's sex discrimination prohibition extends to claims of discrimination based on gender identity..."[8]

As I write this chapter, a highly charged national debate over whether or not transgender people should be allowed to use public restrooms according to their "gender identity" is being publicized. In March of 2016, North Carolina's "Public Facilities Privacy and Security Act," which restricts the use of public bathrooms to biological sex, passed in the state House 82-26 and in the state Senate 32-0. In May of 2016, the U.S. Department of Justice (DOJ) demanded that the state scrap the bill, claiming it violated the 1964 Civil Rights Act. North Carolina refused and now the state and the DOJ have sued each other.

Just how far and how long will we allow our most historical Civil Rights Act to be perverted into something never intended by those who fought so hard to see it enacted?

The Sleeping Giant

When God woke me up, in the spring of 2004, with the question, "Sodom or Salem?" I did not comprehend, at the time, the significance of *the manner* in which He spoke to me. He literally woke me up! It didn't dawn on me until a few years later that my falling off to sleep was symbolic of the condition of the Church in America. Even after I was awakened by His voice and His probing question, I quickly fell right back to sleep.

Indeed, the Church in America is a "sleeping giant." We have the power to change America's future! God is mercifully endeavoring to wake us up! The question is, will we wake up, rise up, and use our power?

The British statesman, Edmund Burke, said it best: "All that is necessary for evil to triumph is for good men to do nothing."[9] Our freedoms came with a great price. They should be guarded with great vigilance. But, at this point in our history, they must be recovered urgently with great vehemence!

I titled chapter one of this book, "My Wake-up Call." But to be honest, I didn't really wake up then. I was stirred up a bit, but not really to action. I mean, not like I was called to war!

Just now I looked at my clock. Do you know what time it is? Right now, as I am writing, it is 4:43 a.m. I woke up without an alarm around 4:00 a.m. to get up and work on this book. This has become a pattern for me. Why? Because I am awake!

In the next chapter I explain what *really* woke me up.

Chapter 7
The Children!

I dared to pray, "Lord, break my heart for what breaks Yours." A couple of years after what I called "my wake-up call," that prayer was answered. I watched some clips on the Internet from the film, "It's Elementary." This film, produced by gay activists, has been shown in thousands of public school classrooms across the country since 1996. (Twenty years before the U.S. Supreme Court decision on same-sex marriage.) It is still being used, along with an updated workbook, to train educators on how to address "anti-gay prejudice." It includes actual classroom footage of elementary school kids being indoctrinated with LGBT propaganda.

The film shows one elementary school in Massachusetts holding their annual Gay and Lesbian Pride Day. A photo display of gay and lesbian families was featured in the hallway. They held a school assembly where everyone sang, "This Little Light of Mine" and some of the faculty members "came out" - they got up in front of the kids and let them know they were gay, each of them receiving an approving applause. In one classroom, children were shown pictures of famous people who are gay, lesbian, and bisexual. Familiar songs, written or performed by gay artists, were played for the children and the kids were asked to guess the names of the artists. Then, they were told these performers were gay.

I lay in bed unable to sleep the night after I viewed "It's Elementary." I was crying and repenting to God for allowing this to happen on my watch in my country. I couldn't get the children's faces out of my mind! Innocent, unsuspecting children were taught in the most manipulative ways imaginable that it is okay to be gay, and that it is wrong and "homophobic" for any one, including parents or religious leaders, to have any level of discomfort or disapproval of gays or lesbians - using racism as a comparison. The truth concerning the most important and fundamental institution of society - the family - was craftily perverted. My heart was broken.

I thought about one little fifth grader in the film named Brandon, who was brave enough to admit, "People say that I act like a girl and sometimes... (he paused, struggling with embarrassment)... I sometimes do." I worried about Brandon. As I lay in bed crying, I calculated that he would now be 18 years old. I wondered if he was now living a gay lifestyle and I could not help feeling personally responsible because of my lack of action on his behalf.

In 2008, my fears were realized. The "Respect for All Project" reissued the "It's Elementary" documentary along with a guidebook, which featured a follow-up of some of the students in the original film. Sure enough, Brandon was one of the "voices of change" who testified how he "came out" after hearing from the teachers at his school that it was "okay to be gay." He was now the head of the Gay-Straight Alliance at his college. I have been "awake" ever since!

Respect for All?

I recently viewed the feature-length documentary, "It's Elementary," again, in its entirety, as well as the sequel, "That's a Family." I couldn't help noticing how parental rights and religious freedoms were disregarded. A third grade class listened as Emily read her Mother's Day essay about her two moms. Included in her essay was a story about a boy in her class who wasn't allowed to come to her house because Emily's parents were lesbians. She said, "I called the boy's house and his mom told me their version of the Bible. I stood up for my mothers. I am proud of my moms and enjoy marching in the gay pride parade every single year with my moms!" The class was then asked by their gay teacher to applaud Emily.

In the accompanying guidebook that came out in 2008, teachers are instructed to consistently use the more inclusive term "LGBT" rather than "gay," but to respect other terms that individuals choose to describe themselves, including "queer, questioning, same-gender-loving, and pansexual."[1] The guidebook also teaches educators how to incorporate LGBT-inclusive material into all subjects at all grade levels.

The expressed motto of the project is "Respect for all" - their expressed purpose is to prevent prejudice, stereotyping, and name-calling. Ironically, the curriculum calls anyone who has "any level of discomfort or disapproval" of people perceived to be LGBT, "homophobic," and asserts that their disapproval "often leads to bias, hatred, and harassment of LGBT people."[2]

The "discomfort or disapproval" in the guidebook's definition of homophobia is of "LGBT people." Of course, nothing is said of their sexual *behavior,* when in fact, the "discomfort" experienced by Christians is not of individuals, but is of immoral sexual *behavior.* And the "disapproval" of Christian parents and Christian leaders is not aimed at "LGBT people"; rather, it is specifically aimed at LGBT sexual *behavior,* which the Bible prohibits for our good.[3] Adherence to God's word does not make a person homophobic or prejudice.

The guidebook addresses how to answer a child who says, "Some people believe that being lesbian, gay, bi-sexual, or transgender is sin."[4] Notice how the comment is phrased: "Some people believe that *being* lesbian, gay..." The classroom discussions in the film are framed around accepting or not accepting "LGBT people," rather than approving or disapproving of their sexual behavior. The guidebook's suggested response to the child's comment includes this remark: "Some people belong to churches, synagogues, mosques, and temples that accept LGBT people and some do not."[5] The response implies that people who belong to churches, synagogues, mosques, and temples that accept homosexual behavior as normal are okay - they're not prejudice; but, people who belong to churches, synagogues, mosques, and temples who believe homosexual behavior is sinful are among those who are homophobic and prejudice.

Ramifications of Legalizing Sodomy

In 2003, a few months after the Supreme Court ruled that state anti-sodomy laws were unconstitutional, Massachusetts became the first state to legalize same-sex marriage. Public schools in Massachusetts held school-wide assemblies to celebrate same-sex marriage, allowing teachers to "come out" and announce whom they would "marry," and by the following year comprehensive LGBT curricula was introduced into the elementary schools.[6]

Ironically, the arguments Justice Anthony Kennedy used when he wrote the majority opinion in the ruling that legalized sodomy, included these two statements: *"The petitioners are entitled to respect for their private lives,"* and *"The present case does not involve minors."*[7] But, their landmark decision essentially "legitimized" homosexual sex, which opened the door to the legalization of same sex marriage - which is obviously not private and ultimately does involve minors.

Kindergarteners in Massachusetts were given picture books telling them that same-sex couples are just another kind of family, like their own parents. Second graders were read a book called *"King and King,"* about two men who have a romance and marry each other. When David Parker, a parent of a kindergartener, insisted on being notified before teachers discuss homosexuality, he was arrested. Yes, this actually happened in the United States of America! He respectfully refused to leave the school property until he was assured that he would receive notification before another lesson on homosexuality was introduced to his five-year-old. For that, he was locked up in jail overnight.[8]

In 2006, David Parker, along with other concerned parents, filed a lawsuit to force notification. The Supreme Court of Massachusetts ruled that parents do not have the right to be notified or opt their children out. The Court's opinion stated that because same-sex marriage is now legal, the school actually has a duty to teach the students that homosexual marriage is equal to heterosexual marriage.[9]

In 2010, Fox News reported that the Helena, Washington school system introduced a "comprehensive sex education" plan for students in kindergarten through 12th grade. First and second graders would be taught that some people grow up to love the same gender, and according to the draft proposal, fifth graders should *"understand that intercourse includes but is not limited to vaginal, oral, or anal penetration."*[10]

In January 2014, the "floodgates" were opened through child-targeting television networks when The Disney Channel introduced its first gay characters on an episode of *Good Luck Charlie*: a lesbian couple (two moms) named Susan and Cheryl appeared with son, Taylor.

And what about middle school and high school students?

In March 2000, the Gay, Lesbian, and Straight Education Network (GLSEN) of Massachusetts held its 10 Year Anniversary GLESEN/Boston Conference at Tufts University. This conference was fully supported by the Massachusetts Department of Education, the Safe Schools Program, the Governor's Commission on Gay and Lesbian Youth, and some presenters even received federal money. During the conference, workshop leaders led a "youth only, ages 14-21" session and spoke about "fisting," a dangerous sexual practice. During the same workshop, an activist asked 14 year old students, "Spit or swallow?... Is it rude?"[11]

In 2005, World Net Daily reported that The Gay Lesbian Straight Education Network sponsored an event at a Boston

High School and distributed a booklet entitled *"The Little Black Book, Queer in the 21ˢᵗ Century"* that included graphic descriptions of homosexual conduct, instructions on how to put on condoms, and a list of gay bars and clubs in the Boston area "for the discerning queerboy."[12]

Please note that everything I've shared in the last few paragraphs took place *before* the 2015 Supreme Court ruling "legalizing" same-sex marriage in every state. Ask yourself what is happening now in public schools and in the entertainment industry!

The emphasis on transforming our culture has now moved over to the "T" in LGBT and a Q has been added – LGBTQ – so adolescents who are "questioning" their sexual orientation will be sure to feel included in the group.

Washington State has announced that schools will be teaching students as young as kindergarten about "gender identity" in the fall of 2017. A Minnesota K-12 charter school also decided to teach their kindergarteners about "gender identity" in order to support a student who is "gender nonconforming" and to "celebrate differences" and "the beauty of being themselves." One of the books the kindergarten teacher would be reading to five and six-year-old students is *My Princess Boy,* a book about a boy who likes to dress in girls' clothing and do "girly" things.[13]

The Battle Over Bathrooms

Even more heated than the North Carolina bathroom law, is the current battle over the use of bathrooms, locker rooms, and showers in public schools. This year (2016), a transgender teen (born a girl, identifying as a boy) in Virginia sued Gloucester High School for their policy that students use bathrooms according to their biological sex, refusing to be restricted to the use of a unisex bathroom. A federal appeals court in Richmond sided with the teen, deferring to the U.S. Education Department's interpretation of discrimination based on "sex" in Title IX to be "gender identity."[14]

On May 14, 2016, a joint letter from the Departments of Education and Justice went out to schools stating that schools should allow transgender students to use bathrooms and other sex-segregated facilities consistent with their "gender identity" and staff should address them by their preferred names and pronouns. The letter asserts that, "gender identity is protected under Title IX,"[15] essentially threatening to withhold federal funding if schools do not comply with the administration's interpretation of the law.

Texas Governor Greg Abbot, who endorsed North Carolina's law, immediately took a stand against the administration's guidelines. He tweeted: "Texas is fighting this. Obama can't rewrite the Civil Rights Act. He's not a king." Lt. Gov. Dan Patrick also publicly denounced the executive overreach, flatly rejecting the President's threats, saying, "In Texas, he can keep his thirty pieces of silver; we will not sell out our children to the federal government."[16]

Lt. Governor Patrick observed that the administration's policy brought to light the biggest issue facing families and schools in America since prayer was taken out of public schools, and predicted that if it prevailed in Court, parents will demand to take their tax dollars and use them to put their children in private schools. He pointed out that this concern is shared by both democrats and republicans and emphatically asserted: "Parents of 14-year-old girls are not going to send their girls to school to shower with 14 year old boys. It's not going to happen!"[17]

Tony Perkins, President of the Family Research Council, likewise reacted: "Never underestimate the outrage of a country in a debate where the safety of innocent children hang in the balance."[18]

I hope Lt. Gov. Patrick's and Tony Perkins' predictions are right.

Christian Education?

In 2015, my home state of Nevada passed legislation allowing for an Educational Savings Account (ESA) Program, which provides a means for parents to choose an alternative to public school. Nevada's governor, Brian Sandoval, signed the legislation into law. The ESA program allows Nevada's parents to use a percentage of state funds for their child's public education toward a private school of their choice. As a result, several Nevada students were happily enrolled in our private school, Word of Life Christian Academy, for the 2015-2016 school year. However, a few families in Nevada, with the help of the ACLU and another advocacy group, have sued the state of Nevada, arguing that Nevada's constitution calls for "uniformity" and that public money should not be used for "religious purposes." Albeit, the funds are not distributed to schools directly, and the state does not favor or disfavor any religion; the ESA simply allows parents to determine their child's specific educational needs and decide where and how to use their child's state educational dollars.

In January of this year (2016), a Carson City judge ruled in favor of the ACLU. Thankfully, the state of Nevada appealed the ruling, sending the case to the Nevada Supreme Court. As I am writing, the high court hearings are scheduled for July 29th, 2016. During the litigation, however, ESA funds were suspended, affecting over 5,000 Nevada students, including several of our students who had to leave WLCA mid-school year.

"Coincidently," in January of this year, I visited Quebec, Canada for the first time. I was invited to speak at a women's conference, where French-speaking ladies came from all over the province to participate and listen to me speak through an interpreter. Although the majority of Quebecers identify as Catholic, less than six percent of them attend mass. Only seven percent are Protestant and less than one percent of Quebecers are evangelical Christians.[19] Understandably, these Christian women jump at the opportunity for fellowship and inspiration, and gladly travel for miles to get together for such an event.

While on this "mission field," only a short plane ride away from home, I heard heart-breaking stories from mothers regarding their children's education. I learned how Quebec's school system, which was Catholic only decades ago, is now completely secularized. Quebec law requires all schools, including those that are "private," to comply with "uniform" standards. Hence, all students are required to attend courses where pro-LGBT and anti-Christian viewpoints are taught, and parents are left without options. I couldn't help but shudder at the potential ramifications of "Common Core" curriculum in the United States.

In addition to the "uniform" standards in their grade schools, Quebec offers the freshman year of college "tuition free." I listened to one mother grieve over her son whom she said was "on fire for God" as a teenager, but was systematically "brain washed" of his Christian beliefs and values during his "free" freshman year of college.

Needless to say, I became fervent in my prayers for the Nevada Supreme Court to rule in favor of the ESA program, which, by the way, will affect 18 other states considering similar legislation.

The Tipping Point

It is recorded in three of the four Gospels that Jesus said it would be better to have a millstone tied around your neck and be thrown into the sea than to offend a child or cause him to sin.[20] Do you know what a millstone is? I like to show people pictures I have taken of 2,000-year-old millstones in Israel. A millstone is a huge, circular tool made from stone that's used for grinding grain, weighing up to 300 pounds!

In the Genesis account of the story of Sodom and Gomorrah, the angels gave Lot the same explanation that the Lord gave Abraham as to why destruction would come to the cities of the plain: *"Because the outcry against Sodom and Gomorrah is great, and their sin is very grave." (Genesis 18:20, 19:13)* According to Webster's Dictionary, an outcry is "an expression or reaction of strong anger or disapproval, a loud cry of vehement protest."[21] The Message Bible says, *"The cries of the victims in Sodom and Gomorrah are deafening."*

The victims? I am convinced that the tipping point in the story of Sodom and Gomorrah was the cries of the children! God, in His mercy, would not allow another generation to arise from those cities.

I'm also convinced that God is demanding a choice from each of us who are eligible voters and citizens of a constitutional republic. Will we choose Sodom or Salem? Like King Bera, will we reject the light we have been granted, ignore the warnings we've been given, and do little or nothing to change the direction of our nation? Or will we choose Salem? Will we respond appropriately to the light we have been granted, heed the warnings we've been given, and fulfill our God-given duty to elect leaders who will represent us – who will respect our Judeo-Christian heritage, and then hold them responsible to protect our religious freedoms and our parental rights?

The souls of our children, and the soul our nation, are hanging in the balance!

Chapter 8
Let the Pulpits Thunder!

In the days of the American Revolution, founding father John Adams pleaded, "Let the pulpits thunder against oppression!" During the anti-slavery movement, Senator Charles Sumner, speaking to ministers, quoted John Adams and pleaded for the pulpits to "thunder again!"[1]

Why did John Adams and Charles Sumner plead with ministers to "let the pulpits thunder?" Because they understood how powerful the pulpits were in influencing the hearts and minds of the people and ultimately shaping the nation. During the Founding Era in our nation, "election sermons" that addressed current issues from a Biblical viewpoint were typically published in local newspapers before elections.

Our nation is presently in a crisis, indeed a cultural and moral war. Ignorance and intimidation have kept the church silent for far too long! Let's be honest: many preachers are paralyzed by fear. The giant bully of "political correctness" and secular humanistic ideology has dominated the landscape. As a result, Christians are not equipped to speak the truth in love to their co-workers, relatives, and friends; much less are they equipped to protect their religious freedoms.

Sodom or Salem? America, It's Your Choice

Talking Points

Political think tanks strategize the most effective informational attack on a particular topic and launch "talking points" - short statements to be used repeatedly within media outlets to saturate the discourse and frame the debate in favor of their agenda. For some activists, the purpose of their talking points is to propagandize, using the technique of "argumentum ad nauseam," i.e., continuous repetition, until the talking points are accepted as facts. When famous and influential people are heard repeatedly making the same statement it is considered "proof by assertion." Never mind whether or not these statements are true; if they are repeated enough times, they are eventually believed to be facts.

For example, in a 2012 Gallop Poll, approximately 3.4% of American adults identified themselves as being lesbian, gay, bisexual, or transgender (LGBT). In July 2014, in the first large-scale government survey measuring Americans' sexual orientation, the National Health Interview Survey (NHIS) reported that only 1.6% of Americans identify as gay or lesbian, and 0.7% as bisexual. But, according to a Gallup Poll conducted May 6-8, 2015, *the American public estimates* on average that 23% of Americans are gay or lesbian! [2]

Why do Americans perceive the percentage to be far higher than the actual facts? The overestimation is clearly a reflection of the high visibility of activists who have pushed the LGBT agenda, and one of their unsubstantiated talking points is "10% of Americans are gay." Add that to the even more prominent media portrayals of gay characters on television and in movies, and you bring the average public estimation up to 23% - when in fact it is significantly less than 4%! The Gay and Lesbian Alliance Against Defamation (GLAAD) issued a report boasting that "TV hasn't merely reflected the changes in social attitudes; it has also had an important role in bringing them about."[3]

In contrast, statistics reveal that the majority of Americans still believe in God. In fact, the majority of Americans still claim to be Christians. In May of 2015, BBC News reported that Pew Research Center found 71% of Americans identifying themselves as Christian. In July of 2015, an ABC News/Belief net poll reported 83% of Americans identifying themselves as Christian. Forty-five percent of Christians in America call themselves Born Again Christians according to the Barna Group, Ventura, California, USA.[4]

Just imagine the impact we could have on our nation if only a fraction of those professing to be Christians were as actively involved in transforming the culture as those who represent less than 4% of the population!

Not a People Fight

As I was leaving Las Vegas yesterday to spend a couple of days away to work on this book, I wondered what to do about not having a mouse for my laptop. (Apparently I lost mine on our last ministry trip.) A friend called me just as I merged onto I-15 toward California. She suggested I stop at the dog-friendly Apple Store in Town Square on my way out of town to purchase the new "magic mouse." (I had my Labrador with me and it's too hot in Vegas to leave him in the car.) Perfect idea.

Of course my dog, Cash, was excited to make the stop and stroll through Town Square. We met a lot of friendly smiles as we walked, and one of the couples we passed on the sidewalk on our way to the Apple Store happened to be a pair of gay men walking hand in hand. I glanced up at them and smiled. Then, one of them asked, "What kind of dog?" (Although a purebred, Cash is much stockier than the typical Lab.) "Chocolate Lab," I responded. More friendly smiles and expressions were exchanged.

As insignificant as this encounter may seem, I decided to share it because I want you to understand that in spite of how passionate I am about waking up the Church to our civic responsibility, I am not angry with or afraid of people living a homosexual lifestyle. Many of us have relatives, friends, or co-workers identifying as gay, lesbian, bisexual, or transgender. I believe everyone deserves to be treated with respect because, like me, they are human beings whom God created and loves.

What's more, as Christians we are called to be merciful! One dictionary defines mercy as "kindness in excess of what might be expected." This is how Jesus treated sinners, like the five-time divorced woman who was living with a man, whom Jesus spoke to by the well in Samaria,[5] and like Zacchaeus, the despised tax-collector, whose home Jesus visited in Jericho,[6] and like the woman caught in the act of adultery and brought by the Pharisees to Jesus. Jesus responded, *"He that is without sin among you, let him first cast a stone at her."*[7]

Mercy is getting what we don't deserve. Jesus demonstrated His mercy toward us in the greatest way imaginable when He died for us when none of us deserved it. Then He put His love in our hearts by the Holy Spirit so we would be able to show others His unconditional love.[8]

The women's ministry of our church in Las Vegas, Ladies LIFEstyles, has an outreach to the women in the "entertainment industry" on the Las Vegas strip called "Agape." Agape is the New Testament Greek word translated love (or "charity" in the KJV). It specifically refers to God's unconditional, extravagant love. Each month we wrap up gifts (nail polish, jewelry, chocolates, etc.) and an Agape Outreach team takes hundreds of these gifts of unconditional love to the strip clubs to present to the exotic dancers. Over the years, we have gained favor with the "bouncers" and the "house moms" who welcome us and escort us to the dressing rooms to present our gifts, along with a specially designed gospel tract *("Girl, Have I Got a Tip for You!")* and a 24-hour hotline number to call for prayer. We now have several former strippers in our church. Others have moved away from Las Vegas and are now leading productive lives. One girl went through Nursing School, graduated at the top of her class, and is now a nurse.

My favorite quote from Evangelist Billy Graham is: "It's the Holy Spirit's job to convict; it's God's job to judge; it's our job to love." (This was his explanation for the warm and gracious manner in which he treated President Bill Clinton during the height of the Clinton scandal when he happened to be seated next to him at the 75th anniversary celebration for Time magazine.)[9]

Christians who are opposed to "gay marriage" and other so-called "anti-discrimination" or "LGBT equality" legislation are often accused of being homophobic or bigoted, when in fact these laws and court rulings often clash with and suppress religious freedoms and parental rights, which merit our opposition. I recently heard a "minister" from a "LGBT inclusive" church accuse mainline Christian pastors of using Scriptures out of context to "oppress" and "persecute" LGBT people, comparing them to the ministers in the 1800's who *opposed* the abolitionist movement.

The Book of Ephesians is no doubt my favorite New Testament Epistle. Watchmen Nee wrote a tremendous commentary on it called *Sit, Walk, Stand*.[10] He points out that in the first part of the letter Paul tells us who we are and what we have in Christ and that we're seated together with Christ in heavenly places. Next, Paul gives instructions on how to walk: walk worthy of our calling, walk not as other gentiles (unbelievers), walk in love, walk as children of light, and walk circumspectly.[11] Finally, "stand, withstand, stand, and stand" is his charge in chapter six.[12]

The Apostle Paul alerts us in Ephesians chapter six that we have an enemy, but reminds us that the enemy is not "flesh and blood." We're fighting, he explains, against *"the rulers of the darkness of this age."*[13] Paul uses the armor of a Roman soldier to illustrate our spiritual warfare and the spiritual armor we must wear for protection. He exhorts us to, first of all, strap on "the belt of truth." The belt in the Roman soldier's armor held all the other pieces of armor in place; interestingly, it also protected his reproductive organs. Without knowing the truth and "wearing it firmly around our waist," we don't stand a chance against the enemy's strategies. And we must be aware that one of the devil's strategies is to lure us into a "people fight."

To the church at Corinth, Paul wrote,

> We are human, but we don't wage war as humans
> do. We use God's mighty weapons, not worldly

weapons, to knock down strongholds of human reasoning and to destroy false arguments. We destroy every proud obstacle that keeps people from knowing God. (2 Corinthians 10:4 NLT)

The Amplified version reads,

For though we walk in the flesh as mortal men, we are not carrying on our spiritual warfare according to the flesh and using the weapons of man. The weapons of our warfare are not physical [weapons of flesh and blood]. Our weapons are divinely powerful for the destruction of fortresses. We are destroying sophisticated arguments and every exalted and proud thing that sets itself up against the true knowledge of God, and we are taking every thought and purpose captive to the obedience of Christ.

Only God's mighty weapons can knock down the "strongholds of human reasoning" that have been erected in people's minds. The Word of God, anointed by the Holy Spirit, is greater and more powerful than any highfalutin man-made idea!

Can We Do More?

On June 12, 2015, just before the U.S. Supreme Court handed down its ruling on same-sex marriage, I received the following letter from Rev. Doug Jones, the Director of the Rhema

Sodom or Salem? America, It's Your Choice

Alumni Association and National Director of Rhema Ministerial Association International (the Bible College my husband and I graduated from and ministerial association through which we're ordained). He was addressing pastors and ministers "from a heart of concern" (the subject title of the email). My own heart-felt sentiments were articulated through his letter. In fact, the Holy Spirit had given me a similar message to preach to ministers at a conference the following week and I introduced my message by reading Rev. Jones' letter:

To Pastors and Ministers:

I normally do not say much about the deterioration of humanity's values within our world. As Christians we have been forewarned about such things in Romans chapter 1, so I am never surprised at what seems to be the next boundary breach of moral decline within today's world. We are also instructed by Paul, to "continue thou in the things which thou hast learned" in spite of how deep the world sinks. (Read the entire chapter of II Timothy 3.)

However, I must admit that I am taken back at the speed of cultural change within today's society. In the last decade the speed of change from what use to be unmentionable to being acceptable is mind-boggling. Especially when compared to the speed of cultural change of like things during my parents and grandparent's lifetime.

So much of this is causing our young people to question their sexual orientation.

Today, the means used to persuade the masses that unacceptable behavior is now acceptable seems to be from our elected leaders, media moguls creating TV series modeling the next lifestyle that they deem acceptable, 'updated' school curriculum and liberal religious leaders publicizing their positional statements.

What kindled this email? Last night, while waiting for the new Jurassic World movie to begin, I was shocked to witness two commercials that introduced the new ABC Family TV reality show called "Becoming Us". It began running last Monday and it is a reality show designed by a teenager to help other kids deal with their fathers becoming a woman.

Is it just me, or does it not seem that there is an unleashed frenzy to bring to the light and legitimize the hidden lifestyles of darkness, that in years past were kept behind closed doors?

Of course we know all of this is directed toward discrediting God's Kingdom in a way that distances us from "Thy kingdom come. Thy will be done in earth, as it is in heaven." God's ways are being challenged in much the same way that Lucifer challenged God's ways as he spoke with Eve in the Garden of Eden. Had Adam guarded the garden, as instructed, the story of mankind would be so very different today...but he failed in his duty.

With the same spirit of instruction given Adam to protect, Paul's instructions to the leaders of Ephesus has never been more important to heed than today (Acts 20:28-31). If ever the church is being inundated with inferior lifestyles and deception it is today!

As ambassadors for God we have been commissioned to "preach the Word"(2 Tim. 4:1-3). "All scripture is given by inspiration of God, and is profitable for doctrine, for reproof..."(2 Tim. 3:16-17). We are admonished to follow the Apostle Paul's example to preach "all the counsel of God" (Acts 20:27).

With all this said:

If there was ever a time for pulpits to impart God's counsel into husbands it is today.
If there was ever a time for pulpits to impart God's counsel into wives it is today.

If there was ever a time for pulpits to impart God's counsel into parents it is today.

If there was ever a time for pulpits to impart God's counsel into youth it is today.

If there was ever a time for pulpits to impart God's counsel into children it is today.

To those of us who may read this and conclude that we have done a good job in these areas, my plea is this: Can we do more? Can we improve on what we have taught our husbands, wives, fathers, mothers, youth and children? Can we focus more attention to pass on God's ways and wisdom to them so that they are thoroughly furnished to shine as lights within this ever-darkening world?

May God's grace fill us with His wisdom as we feed "the flock, over the which the Holy Ghost hath made you overseers" (Acts 20:28).

Serving you as you serve Him,

Doug Jones: RMAI National Director [14]

Five Smooth Stones

In The Book of First Samuel, chapter 17, we find the thrilling story of David and Goliath. Goliath was a big bully. Every day and every night he taunted the children of Israel, challenging them to send a man out into the valley to fight with him. No one was willing to stand up to Goliath. The entire Israelite army was paralyzed with fear.

This is typical of much of today's church!

I understand that it's easy to get dismayed. A "giant bully" has been strutting his stuff for a long time - belittling Christians and accusing anyone who disagrees with him of being a bigot. It seems this "Goliath" has convinced the bulk of Americans, and even some prominent Christian leaders, that we must go along with whatever he says. As Robert Bork observed in his book, *Slouching Toward Gomorrah: Modern Liberalism and American Decline:*

> With each new evidence of deterioration we lament for a moment, and then become accustomed to it. So unrelenting is the assault on our sensibilities that many of us grow numb, finding resignation to be the rational, adaptive response to an environment that is increasingly polluted and apparently beyond our control.[16]

When David showed up in the Valley of Elah to feed his brothers some cheese and bread, he overheard the giant Philistine shouting his threats. The Bible says that all the men of Israel had become dreadfully afraid of Goliath. But, David had been listening to a different tune. He had been spending time on the hillside worshiping God with his harp while tending to his father's sheep. When a wild animal snatched one of the lambs from the fold, he went after it. David had discovered that God's power would show up to help him when he set out to rescue a lamb - he had even been delivered from the paw of a lion and the paw of a bear.

"Who is this uncircumcised Philistine, that he should defy the armies of the living God?" David protested. He promptly volunteered to accept the giant's challenge. *"Is there not a cause?"* He demanded.[17]

When David prepared to fight Goliath, he chose not to wear the armor King Saul offered him because it didn't fit and it wasn't tried. He decided to use weapons he knew were tried and true: age-old stones from the earth, washed by the waters over eons of time. David chose five smooth stones from the brook and ran at the fierce giant with a sling in his hand. He slung one of those smooth stones through the air and struck the Philistine right between his eyes. The stone sunk into Goliath's forehead, knocking him to the ground. What a champion of faith this young David was!

In my next book, *Five Smooth Stones*, I present timeless truths I have chosen from the eternal waters of God's Word for defeating the Goliath of our generation. These "five stones" have the power to demolish the false arguments that have influenced public opinion and intimidated the Church. I urge you to pick them up yourself, and start slinging them at the Goliath "defying the armies of the living God" in your sphere of influence!

Five Smooth Stones:

1. Marriage is a Sacred Covenant Between a Man and a Woman.[18]

2. Sex is Designed Exclusively for Marriage.[19]

3. Homosexuality is not Genetic or Immutable.[20]

4. Gender is Genetic and Immutable.[21]

5. Children are the Responsibility of Parents.[22]

The New Pulpit

A "pulpit" is a platform or a medium to convey a message. In the 1700s and 1800s the church pulpit and the printed page were the primary mediums used to influence the masses.

The 1920s brought radio broadcasting on the scene and several evangelists used this medium to share their message. Sister Aimee Simple McPherson, known for her "illustrated sermons," was the first woman to get a license for radio broadcasting. She stepped up to the "radio pulpit" and caused it to thunder. Billy Graham caused the "crusade pulpit" and "television pulpit" to thunder for several decades during the 20th Century, as did many others.

As mentioned in chapter 6, during the 1950s and 1960s, Dr. Martin Luther King Jr. used the power of his pulpit, which was not confined to the four walls of his church, to change the American culture and, indeed, even the law.

As a matter of fact, every one of us has a sphere of influence - each of has a "pulpit" of some shape and size. If you're willing to step up to yours with a message of truth from God's word, God will cause your pulpit to thunder, and perhaps even emit some light into our darkened culture.

Today's technology affords us a great variety of media outlets, including television, movies, the Internet, and social media. I have been thrilled to witness the "movie pulpit" thunder recently with films like "Heaven is For Real," "God's Not Dead," "War Room," and "Miracles from Heaven." Regarding War Room's phenomenal box office success, CNN said, "some might call it a faith-based David versus the secular Goliaths in the entertainment industry."[15]

Is There Not a Cause?

David exclaimed, *"Is there not a cause?"* The young people in America, and even in our churches, are growing up confused about what marriage is, what a family is, and who they are! Beyond that, Christians are clueless when it comes to defending their religious freedoms!

Goliath (AKA secular humanism, modern liberalism, LGBT activism, academia elitism, and political correctness) is challenging our religious rights, our parental rights, and even our freedom of speech. In other nations, including Canada, where same-sex marriage has been legalized, "hate speech" legislation has subsequently been passed, making it illegal to speak out against homosexual practices. This silencing is now being enforced in Europe and in Canada - Christians arrested for quoting the Bible and calling homosexual sex, along with other illicit sexual behavior, sin.

This bullying is not going to stop unless we stand up to it!

Like David, we must care enough about God's lambs to go after the "lions and bears" that have them in their clutches. I'm confident God's power will show up to help us when we do! Like David, a man after God's own heart, we must care enough for God's cause to face and fight the Goliath that is intimidating the people of God! I'm confident that when we do, God's power will direct our efforts and cause these "stones" to hit the giant bully right between the eyes, and set God's people free!

Some people may disagree with what you say. Some may ridicule you. Some may even accuse you of being motivated by fear or hatred. But some people will be set free by the truth you courageously proclaim! And many others will be equipped to vote their Biblical values, as well as step up to their own "pulpits" to speak the truth in love.

I hear the Lord pleading, *"Let the pulpits thunder again!"*

Sodom or Salem?

Sodom

- Hebrew: Burnt (Utter Destruction)
- Judgment
- City of Sin
- Symbolic of Eternal Damnation

Salem

- Hebrew: Peace (Complete Wholeness)
- Jerusalem
- City of God
- Symbolic of Eternal Reward

© 2015

Epilogue
For Such a Time as This

This book is the first of at least three parts to the Sodom or Salem message. The second part is in my next book, *Five Smooth Stones*. The third part contains a more complete and revelatory analogy of America in the story of Sodom and Gomorrah, examining all of the characters, including Lot, who represents the Church, and Abraham, "the character of choice" - a Covenant friend of God who commanded his children, paid his tithes, and interceded before God on behalf of Sodom. The absolute necessity of America standing with Israel and acknowledging Jerusalem (choosing Salem) as Israel's eternal, undivided Capital is also a decisive part of the message.

In *Sodom or Salem? America It's Your Choice*, I primarily focus on one character - the king of Sodom, whom God revealed is the character in the story of Sodom and Gomorrah that we don't have a choice but to identify with because America is a constitutional republic, not a monarchy. After hearing "Sodom or Salem?" the Lord instructed me: "I want you to study the characters in the story, beginning with the king."

I understand that what America need's most is another Great Spiritual Awakening! And that awakening must begin in the Church! I would like to have written this first volume on praying for America, using Abraham as a great example of an intercessor, because I understand that prayer comes first! We must take our place in prayer! Nonetheless, I'm convinced that the message of this book, as well as many other recent and prophetic wake-up calls to the Church, have been given to us in answer to prayer! Moreover, an awakening to God is an awakening to His word!

Therefore, my first assignment after *literally* being awakened out of sleep, and the message I hope you take away from this book, is this: "We the people" are the "king of Sodom," holding the ruling power at a crucial moment in history. Judgment is imminent. The peace, protection, and prosperity we so earnestly desire for our communities and our nation depends not only upon the prayers of God's people, but also upon the active and responsible civic action of God's people.

Given this revelation, and whatever other eye-opening information you may have received from reading this book, I ask you to please ask yourself: If the United States of America were a monarchy and you were privileged to be the king, what would you do to change the direction of this nation? What would your policy priorities be? If you're a Christian, what specific laws do you believe God would want you to enact or enforce? What kind of judges would He want you to appoint? Your answers to these questions are your answers as to how you should vote in the next election and how you should use whatever position of influence you have to make a difference while you have the chance.

When Esther was lacking the courage to step out of her comfort zone and use her position of influence to save her people, she was issued a challenge from her uncle Mordecai, who had raised her:

Do not think in your heart that you will escape

in the king's palace any more than all the other Jews. For if you remain completely silent at this time, relief and deliverance will arise for the Jews from another place, but you and your father's house will perish. Yet who knows whether you have come to the kingdom for such a time as this? (Esther 4:13-14)

As Christians we often hear this passage applied to our purpose in God's kingdom, but let's not forget that it wasn't the kingdom of God, but the kingdom of Persia, that Mordecai was referring to when he provokingly asked Esther to consider her calling.

Likewise, the Apostle Paul not only used his spiritual gifts to advance God's kingdom - he took advantage of his Roman citizenship and stood up to the governmental authorities of his day in order to advance the Gospel of Jesus Christ for his generation.[1]

In The Book of Hebrews, chapter eleven, we read about (and preach about) ordinary people who accomplished amazing things for God by acting in faith. Included in this famous list of faith heroes and faith exploits, we find this verse:

By faith these people overthrew kingdoms, ruled with justice, and received what God had promised them. (Hebrews 11:33)

George Barna is the founder of The Barna Group, a market research firm specializing in studying the religious beliefs and behavior of Americans. He is the most quoted Christian in America. I recently heard him speak to a gathering of Christian leaders regarding the 2016 election. He reported that in the 2012 presidential election, 26 million evangelical Christians did not vote and 12 million evangelical Christians were not even registered to vote.

In chapter 8 of this book, *Let the Pulpits Thunder,* I inserted a letter written to ministers from the director of my ministerial association who posed the question, *"Can we do more?"* Regarding our civic responsibility, I'm posing the same question to eligible voters and citizens of the United States: *Can we do more?*

If you're not registered to vote, will you get registered? (www.usa.gov/register-to-vote)[2] If you are registered to vote, will you examine the records and positions of each local, state, and federal candidate and go to your polling place to vote - not according to a political party affiliation, but for the candidates you believe will best represent your Biblical moral values? Christian voter guides that provide information on where each candidate stands on key issues can be found on various websites including, www.christianvoterguide.com/national-voter-guides and www.afaaction.net.[3]

In addition, would you prayerfully consider running for a public office yourself, or supporting a candidate's campaign with a financial donation, or getting involved in your community on a precinct level, volunteering your time?

If you are a pastor of a church, will you "preach the word" regarding key moral issues affecting this nation? Will you "preach the word" concerning civic responsibility to your congregation? In addition, will you set up a voter registration table in the foyer of your church and encourage your church members to register to vote? Will you also make available to them Christian voter guides?

To summarize the essence of this call to action, I will conclude with Pastor Mac Hammond's endorsement of this book, which I believe really "nails it" (Thank you, Pastor Mac!):

> *Sodom or Salem?* – A choice that Americans will make at the polling place, and that will depend on Christians deciding to no longer be the "silent" majority.

Good read – thanks, Vicki!

Notes and References

Chapter 1: My Wake-Up Call

1. Psalm 76:2

2. Hebrews 7:2-4

3. Psalm 110:4 and Hebrews 5:6, 10; 6:20; 7:11, 17, 21

4. Webster's New World Dictionary. 2nd College ed. 1982. Print

Chapter 2: Degrees of Light

1. Strong, James, and Gordon Lindsay. *Strong's Concordance: Bible Dictionary; Study of the Words of Jesus.* Charlotte, NC: P.T.L. Television Network, 1975. Print.

2. Thompson, Frank Charles. The Thompson Chain-Reference Bible; Compiled and Edited by Frank Charles Thompson. Place of Publication Not Identified: Eyre and Spottiswood, 1964. Print. Archaeological Supplement: Commentary by Dr. George Adam Smith on the ruins of Sodom and Gomorrah

3. Matthew 18:3

4. Romans 7:9

5. John 3:3

6. Genesis 9:29; 2 Peter 2:5

7. Genesis 9:1-17

8. Job chapters 38-41

9. Proverbs 14:12, 16:25 KJV

10. Romans 2:15

11. Romans 3:20

12. Galatians 3:24

13. Leviticus 17:11 & Hebrews 9:22

14. 2 Timothy 3:16

15. Romans 6:23a

16. Romans 6:23b

17. Romans 5:8

18. Romans 10:9

19. EMI Christian Music Publishing, Roberson, Carroll. He's Everything to Me. Bud John Songs, Inc., 1964. Vinyl recording.

Chapter 3: When Judgment Comes

1. Matthew 10:6

2. Matthew 10:8

3. Genesis 19:9

4. Genesis 19:11

5. Genesis 19:14

6. Bond, Alan, and Mark Hempsell. *A Sumerian Observation of the Köfels' Impact Event: A Monograph*. Great Britain: Alcuin Academics, 2008. Print.

7. "U.S. Strategic Bombing Survey: The Effects of the Atomic Bombings of Hiroshima and Nagasaki, June 19, 1946. President's Secretary's File, Truman Papers.". Harry S. Truman Presidential Library and Museum. p. 7. Retrieved January 23, 2016.

8. "10 Things You Didn't Know About the Dead Sea." Twisted Sifter. 24 June 2012. Web. 10 June 2016.

9. "Find Great Places to Stay, Shop, or Visit from Local Ex-

perts." www.Dead Sea.com. Web. 10 June 2016.

Chapter 4: America's Beginnings

1. Columbus, Christopher, and Kay Brigham. Christopher Columbus' Book of Prophecies: Reproduction of the Original Manuscript with English Translation. Barcelona: Libros CLIE, 1991. Print.

2. Ibid. (same source as above)

3. Desmond Wilcox, Ten Who Dared (Boston: Little, Brown and Company, 1977), 45-46.

4. Christopher Columbus, Journal, 1942, quoted in Federer, United States Folder, Library of Classics.

5. Dwight D. Einsenhower, recorded for the "Back-to-God" Program of the American Legion, 20 February 1955, quoted in Federer, United States Folder, Library of Classics.

6. Paul Johnson, A History of the American People (New York: HarperCollins Publishers, 1997), 29-30

7. Interview with Rev. Peter Marshall, on location at Plymouth, MA. Coral Ridge Ministries-TV, Ft. Lauderdale, FL, August, 1989, quoted in Gibbs/ Newcombe, One Nation Under God (Christian Law Association, 2003), 35.

8. Gibbs and Newcombe, One Nation Under God: Ten

Things Every Christian Should Know About the Founding of America, Christian Law Association, 2003. pg. 42-43.

9. Rabbi Daniel Lapin, America's Real War, Multnomah Books, 1999. pg. 128

10. "THE NEW ENGLAND PRIMER." The New England Primer, 1777 Edition. Web. 19 July 2016. www.sacred-texts.com/chr/nep/1777/.

11. New England's First Fruits," 1643, quoted in The Annals of America, Vol. 1,175

12. Benjamin Pierce, A History of Harvard University (Cambridge, MA: Brown, Shattuck, and Company, 1833), p.5, Appendix

13. The Catalogue of the Library of Yale College in New Haven (New London: T. Green, 1743), prefatory remarks; see also The Catalogue of the Library of Yale College in New Haven (New Haven: James Parker, 1755), prefatory remarks.

14. John Witherspoon, The Works of the Reverend John Witherspoon (Philadelphia: William W. Woodward, 1802), Vol III, p. 42, from "The Dominion of Providence over the Passions of Men," May 17, 1776.

15. Gibbs and Newcombe, One Nation Under God: Ten

Things Every Christian Should Know About the Founding of America, Christian Law Association, 2003. pg. 67

16. Ibid., pg. 90

17. Ibid., pg. 97

18. The Declaration of Independence

19. January-3 February 2002 National Weekly Edition, The Washington Times, 28.

20. Quoted in Titus, God, Man, and Law, 42.

21. Quoted in Ibid, 43.

22. Wilson, Vol. I, pp. 120, 137-138, "Of the Law of Nature."

23. The Declaration of Independence, World Almanac, 513

Chapter 5: We the People
1. The Preamble to the Constitution

2. Benjamin Hart, Faith and Freedom: The Christian Roots of American Liberty, Lewis & Stanley, 1990. pg. 330.

3. Ibid., pg. 227.

4. Ibid., pg. 228.

5. Butler, Keith. Reviving the American Spirit. Lake Mary, FL: FrontLine, 2006. Print. pg. 121

6. Beliles & McDowell, America's Providential History, pg. 261.

7. Ibid., 241.

8. Quoted in Catherine Drinker Bowen, Miracle at Philadelphia: The Story of the Constitutional Convention May to September 1787 (Boston et al.: An Atlantic Monthly Press Book, a division of Little, Brown and Company, 1966/1986), 61.

9. David Barton, Original Intent: The Courts, The Constitution, & Religion, Wallbuilder Press, 2000, pg. 253

10. Webster's Dictionary definition of federalism: Noun - the federal principle or system of government.

11. Beliles and McDowell, America's Providential History, pg. 190.

12. Ibid., pg. 190.

13. Ibid., pg. 260.

14. Thomas Jefferson, Memoir, Correspondence, and Miscellanies, From the Paper of Thomas Jefferson, Thomas

Jefferson Randolph, editor (Boston: Gray and Bowen, 1830), Vol. IV, p. 374, to Judge William Johnson on June 12, 1823.

15. Read more about the misuse of The Fourteenth Amendment in my next book, *Five Smooth Stones*, Stone #1

16. Phillips, Amber. "John Roberts: Constitution 'Had Nothing to Do with It'." Washington Post. The Washington Post, 26 June 2015. Web. 02 Aug. 2016. https://www.washingtonpost.com/news/the-fix/wp/2015/06/26/john-robertss-full-throated-gay-marriage-dissent-constitution-had-nothing-to-do-with-it/.

17. Tapson, Mark. "Scalia's Full Dissent on Same-Sex Marriage Ruling." Truth Revolt. N.p., 27 June 2015. Web. 02 Aug. 2016. http://www.truthrevolt.org/news/scalias-full-dissent-same-sex-marriage-ruling.

18. Ibid

19. Ibid

20. Marriage laws were based on the origin of the marital union in Genesis. In 1913, the Texas Supreme Court reflected the views of the Founding Fathers when it declared (Marriage was not originated by human law.)

21. "Abraham Lincoln - Liberty Quotes Blog." Liberty-

Quotes. Web. 02 Aug. 2016. http://quotes.libertytree.ca/ quote_blog/Abraham.Lincoln.Quote.4147.

22. David Barton, The Role of Pastors & Christians in Civil Government, Wallbuilder Press, 2008,pg. 35

23. David Barton, Keys to Good Government: According to the Founding Fathers, Wallbuilder Press, 1994, pg. 41

Chapter 6: Wake Up! We're in a War!

1. Robert H. Bork, Slouching Towards Gomorrah: Modern Liberalism and American Decline, Regan Books / Harper Collins Publishing, 1996, pgs. 3-4

2. Robert Stearns: Why Israel Matters, Charisma Mag. Article, May 2006, pg. 48 (Emphasis mine.)

3. Kirk, Marshall, and Erastes Pill. The Overhauling of Straight America, Guide Magazine 1987. http://library.gay-homeland.org/0018/EN/EN_Overhauling_Straight.htm.

4. Grieve, Tim. "Scalia's Blistering Dissent on DOMA." The Atlantic. Atlantic Media Company, 26 June 2013. Web. 15 July 2016. http://www.theatlantic.com/national/archive/2013/06/scalias-blistering-dissent-on-doma/277245/.

5. Sheldon, Louis P. The Agenda. Lake Mary, FL: FrontLine, 2005. Print.

6. New York: Harper & Row, 1964. "Letters from Birmingham" Why We Can't Wait. Print.

7. Ibid. (same source as above)

8. Weatherby, Danielle. "From Jack to Jill" NYU Review of Law Social Change. 10 Aug. 2015. Web. 15 July 2016. https://socialchangenyu.com/volume-39-issue-1/from-jack-to-jill-gender-expression-as-protected-speech-in-the-modern-schoolhouse/.

9. Beliles & McDowell, America's Providential History, pg. 232.

Chapter 7: The Children
1. Chung, Christy, and Michael Courville. It's Elementary: Talking about Gay Issues in School. Harriman, NY: Groundspark, 2008. Print. pg. 5

2. Ibid., pg. 125

3. Exodus 20:14 and Deuteronomy 5:18; Leviticus 18:22-23; Ephesians 5:3-8

4. Chung, Christy, and Michael Courville. It's Elementary: Talking about Gay Issues in School. Harriman, NY: Groundspark, 2008. Print. pg. 52

5. Ibid., pg. 52

6. "What Same-sex 'marriage' Has Done to Massachusetts." http://www.massresistance.org/docs/marriage/effects_of_ssm_2012/

7. Ross, David E. "The Senators and the Gays." Rossde.com. Web. 14 July 2016. http://www.rossde.com/editorials/edtl_senator_gays.html.

8. "David Parker Incident." David Parker Incident. Web. 14 July 2016. http://www.massresistance.org/docs/parker/main.html.

9. US Supreme Court Rejects David Parker's Appeal. 7 Oct. 2008. Web. 14 July 2016. http://www.massresistance.org/docs/parker_lawsuit/sc_petition/rejected.html.

10. Sedlak, James W., M.S. "Children Exposed to Montana Sex-Ed." Children Exposed to Montana Sex-Ed. Web. 15 July 2016. http://www.christiannewswire.com/news/89114396.html.

11. Hoft, Jim. "Obama's School Czar." Breitbart News. 21 June 2011. Web. 15 July 2016. http://www.breitbart.com/big-government/2011/06/21/good-riddanceobamas-radical-safe-schools-czar-hits-the-skids/.

12. Little Black Book. Web. 15 July 2016. http://www.mass-

resistance.org/docs/issues/black_book/black_book_in-side.html.

13. "Gender Identity' for 5 & 6 Year Olds." Breitbart News. 01 Mar. 2016. Web. 15 July 2016. http://www.breitbart. com/big-government/2016/03/01/school-forces-gender-identity-5-year-olds/.

14. "Federal Appeals Court Sides with Transgender Teen." RSS. 19 Apr. 2016. Web. 15 July 2016. http://www.lg-btinstitute.org/news/2016/4/19/federal-appeals-court-sides-with-transgender-teen-says-bathroom-case-can-go-forward.

15. Emanuella Grinberg. "W.H. Issues Guidance on Transgender Bathrooms." CNN. Cable News Network, 14 May 2016. Web. 20 July 2016. http://www. cnn.com/2016/05/12/politics/transgender-bathrooms-obama-administration/.

16. Healy, Jack, and Richard PÉrez-peÑa. "Solace and Fury as Schools React to Transgender Policy." The New York Times. The New York Times, 13 May 2016. Web. 15 July 2016. http://www.nytimes.com/2016/05/14/us/transgen-der-bathrooms.html?_r=0.

17. Ibid: (same source as above)

18. "Tony Perkins: President Obama's 'Transgender Agen-

da'" Joe.My.God. 28 May 2016. Web. 15 July 2016. http://www.joemygod.com/2016/05/28/tony-perkins-president-obamas-transgender-agenda-is-one-the-big-gest-miscalculations-of-his-tenure/.

19. Hovsepian, Ann-Margret. "Quebec: Canada's Prodigal Province." ChristianityToday.com. 22 May 2012. Web. 15 July 2016. http://www.christianitytoday.com/ct/2012/may/quebec-prodigal-province.html.

20. Scriptures: Mark 9:42, Matthew 18:6, Luke 17:2

21. Webster's New World Dictionary. 2nd College ed. 1982. Print

Chapter 8: Let the Pulpits Thunder

1. Beliles & McDowell, America's Providential History, pg. 232.

2. "Americans Greatly Overestimate Percent Gay, Lesbian in U.S." Gallup.com. 6-8, May 2015. Web. 13 July 2016. http://www.gallup.com/poll/183383/americans-greatly-overestimate-percent-gay-lesbian.aspx.

3. Bozell III, L. Brent. "TV Has to Be at Least 42 Percent Gay?" 25 Oct. 2013. Web. 14 July 2016. https://cnsnews.com/commentary/l-brent-bozell-iii/tv-has-be-least-42-percent-gay.

4. Barna Survey Reveals Significant Growth in Born Again Population." Barna Group., 26 Mar. 2006. Web. 02 Aug. 2016. <https://www.barna.org/component/content/article/5-barna-update/45-barna-update-sp-657/157-barna-survey-reveals-significant-growth-in-born-again-population#.V6EYUvkrK9I>

5. John 4:13-18

6. Luke 19:1-10

7. John 8:3-11

8. Romans 5:5

9. Greene, Steve, Dr. "Billy Graham: A Faithful Witness." Charisma Magazine July 2005. Print.

10. Nee, Watchman. Sit, Walk, Stand. Wheaton, IL: Tyndale House, 1977. Print.

11. Ephesians 4:1,17, Ephesians 5:2

12. Ephesians 6:11-14

13. Ephesians 6:12

14. Letter from Doug Jones, Director of the Rhema Alumni Association and National Director of Rhema Ministerial

Association International, dated June 12th, 2015. Used by permission.

15. France, Lisa R. "How 'War Room' Is Winning the Battle of the Box Office." CNN. Cable News Network, 8 Sept. 2015. Web. 13 July 2016. http://www.cnn.com/2015/09/08/entertainment/war-room-box-office-feat/.

16. Bork, Robert H. Slouching towards Gomorrah: Modern Liberalism and American Decline. New York: Regan, 1996. Print.

17. 1 Samuel 17:26, 29

18. Mark 10:5-9, Ephesians 5:31-32, Hebrews 13:4

19. Romans 1:24-27, 1 Corinthians 6:9-11, 18, Ephesians 5:3-7, Colossians 3:5-6

20. Romans 1:16, 1 Corinthians 6:9-11, 2 Corinthians 5:17

21. 1 Corinthians 6:19-20, 2 Corinthians 5:10-11

22. Ephesians 6:1-4, Colossians 3:20-21

Epilogue
1. Acts 22:25-30, 25:7-11

2. https://www.usa.gov/register-to-vote

3. http://www.christianvoterguide.com/national-voter-guides, http://votesmart.org/, http://www.afaaction.net.

Sodom or Salem?

America, It's Your Choice

By Vicki Shearin

STUDY QUESTIONS

Chapter 1: My Wake-Up Call

1. Lot chose to journey in the direction of Sodom because it was a "well watered plain." What can we learn about Lot's decision?

2. In what ways does Melchizedek typify Christ?

3. Describe King Bera's encounter with Abraham. Was his response to Abraham and Melchizedek appropriate?

4. What is the allegory drawn from the story in Genesis chapter 14? How does King Bera symbolize the citizens of the United States?

Chapter 2: Degrees of Light

1. What does the story of Sodom and Gomorrah teach us about when judgment will come?

2. God has provided mankind many different ways to know right from wrong. How does the light of conscience and the light of creation help us to discern God's will?

3. How does the Light of Commandment make Christians today even more responsible for their sins than Sodom and Gomorrah?

4. How has God touched or transformed your life with the Light of the Gospel?

5. As Americans, why do we have such a great responsibility to reach out with the Gospel to others? What sets us apart from the rest of the world?

Chapter 3: When Judgment Comes

1. Lot described the behavior of the men of Sodom to be "wicked." How does their response to Lot correspond to the attitudes of people in America today when confronted with the truth of the God's word?

2. What geological phenomenon stands as evidence for the destruction of Sodom and Gomorrah?

3. The prophets Isaiah, Jeremiah and Ezekiel openly rebuked the Israelites by comparing them to the cities of Sodom and Gomorrah. How do the warnings of the prophets to Israel resemble the events in modern America?

Chapter 4: America's Beginnings

1. What major historical figure is hardly ever recognized as a Christian leader and yet was motivated by his Christian beliefs to explore the New World?

2. What document was created by Separatists? Why is it so important?

3. Why were early settlers so insistent on providing education to everyone? What does this show about the beliefs of the founding fathers of America?

4. How did the clergy of New England help in the Revolutionary War?

Chapter 5: We the People

1. Following the comparison of "The Battle of Four Kings Against Five" to America, what do the slime pits represent?

2. What was the separation of powers, as laid out in the United States Constitution, meant to compensate for?

3. How have the warnings of Thomas Jefferson, in regard to tyranny, come true in America?

4. _____ is to a country what _____ is to an individual.

5. Consider the parable of Matthew 13: 24-30 in conjunction with the rulings of the U. S. Supreme Court. How has "the enemy" sown tares in America?

6. Do you believe that Charles Finney's statements regarding the duty of Christians to their government still apply today?

Chapter 6: Wake Up! We're in a War!

1. What are the "twin threats" to the future of Western civilization?

2. How do the Gay Rights Movement and the Civil Rights Movement differ (specifically looking at their origins)?

3. How has the 14th Amendment been twisted out of its original meaning?

Chapter 7: The Children

1. In an attempt to find "equality" for the LGBT community, what other established constitutional rights have been disregarded in the process?

2. What is the value in distinguishing between the sexual behavior of a person and the person themself?

3. How does Texas Governor Greg Abbot's tweet concerning the misuse of Title IX warn about the overreach of power taking place in the United States?

Chapter 8: Let the Pulpits Thunder

1. What has kept the Church silent in America (particularly about moral issues)?

2. Considering your own experience with the news and other media outlets, how have the talking points of the LGBT community affected your life and way of thinking?

3. Were you surprised by the statistics presented in this chapter? If you were, why do you think there is a disparity between the facts and your perception?

4. Time and time again Jesus comes into contact with sinners. What does his behavior towards sinners teach us about how Christians should act toward those who do not know the Gospel and are living in sin?

5. Why is the "belt of truth" so important to a Christian's stand against sin and immorality?

6. What is your pulpit and how is God calling you to use it for His Glory?

Epilogue:

1. If you're not registered to vote, will you get registered? (www.usa.gov/register-to-vote)[2]

2. If you are registered to vote, will you examine the records and positions of each local, state, and federal candidate and go to your polling place to vote - not according to a political party affiliation, but for the candidates you believe will best represent your Biblical moral values? (Christian voter guides that provide information on where each candidate stands on key issues can be found on various websites including, www.christianvoterguide.com/national-voter-guides, www.afaaction.net.) [3]

3. In addition, would you prayerfully consider running for a public office yourself, or supporting a candidate's campaign with a financial donation, or getting involved in your community on a precinct level, volunteering your time?

4. If you are a pastor of a church, will you "preach the word" regarding key moral issues affecting this nation? Will you "preach the word" concerning civic responsibility to your congregation?

5. In addition, if you are a pastor, will you set up a voter registra-

tion table in the foyer of your church and encourage your church members to register to vote? Will you also make available to them Christian voter guides?

About The Author

Vicki Shearin, alongside her husband, David, are the founders and pastors of Word of Life Christian Center, a non-denominational, multi-cultural church in Las Vegas, Nevada. The church began with five people in 1982 and has grown to over 2000 members with various outreaches, including an international television ministry, *The Word for Living*. In addition, they founded Word of Life Bible Institute and Word of Life Christian Academy, a Pre-K through 12th grade school, winning awards in athletics, robotics, and the arts.

Vicki has a passionate message to women about living in the "last days" of Bible prophecy - a time in which God is raising up a great host of women to pray and publish His Word (Psalm 68:11). She is the director of Ladies LIFE*styles*, which includes